WILDLY UNBROKEN

Jasmine Waldegrave

Inspiring Faith

Wildy UnBroken: Live your blessed life while it's all falling apart

by Jasmine Waldegrave

Published by Inspiring Faith

www.inspiringfaithonline.com

Copyright © 2022 Jasmine Waldegrave

For permissions contact the author at
www.inspiringfaithonline.com/contact-us

ISBN: 978-1-8381245-1-9

Cover by Angelee van Allman

To Karl,

This is for you, my Wildly Unbroken adventuring partner, with all my love. Your sheer grit and determination are inspiring to everyone you meet. You have never stopped believing, never stopped taking ground and have consistently encouraged me to keep going.

CONTENTS

PREFACE

Blessing, it is something we all want, something we seek, and a familiar word that slips off the Christian tongue all too easily. But what is it really, and how do we walk in it? Is it a destination we get to when we have become good enough Christians, or simply the visible evidence of the favour of God in our lives? I suspect that these are rather simplified views of blessing. In reality, I believe that the truth of understanding blessing and living the blessed life is more of a journey of discovery taken with God into the very core of our beings. The journey will look different for every adventurer into his Word, but it is a quest that holds treasure far richer than anything the world can offer. This book is my journey of discovering what it truly means to live in the wild and untamed blessing of God, while at the same time navigating a very painful and difficult season of life. I hope that as you follow along with my journey, you too will discover what it means to live your untamed life in all its fullness. A life lived Wildly Unbroken!

INTRODUCTION

'Yes'

This story starts with one very powerful word. It's a word uttered so simply by so many, but changes everything that happens after it. The word was 'yes.' That word followed the cliff edge question of, 'Will you marry me?' It was a question I never thought I would hear, and if I am honest never sought to find. I was 19 years old, chronically ill with M.E., and mostly confined to the house because of the severe pain and fatigue that had been my almost constant companion for close on three years. But the handsome young man before me could see beyond that and still wanted to marry me.

I had known Karl since childhood, from when I had shyly peered past my youth camp leader's shoulder at the new face before me. He was a good friend of my older sister, and a young leader at the Bible camp where I was an attendee. I had been a shy and quiet girl, who preferred reading a book to sports, and would rather avoid anything that looked remotely risky or dangerous. I was a huge fan of rules, order, and ensuring that I conformed to both. Karl loved books too, but he loved nature and the outdoors more. We both loved Jesus. As our friendship and faith grew over the years, he went to university and qualified with a degree in Nature Conservation. By the time I was 18, Karl had worked with the wildlife of Africa while I, on the other hand, had moved to the UK from South Africa with my British parents. But the hand of God had always been on our friendship, and when Karl decided to take a gap year to visit the UK everything changed. I was no longer the young girl from Bible camp, and he was no longer in the wild of Africa. A new wild adventure lay before us, but the key to the door to that adventure was one small word.

That small 'yes' changed everything for us. It opened the door to the excitement of dreaming the impossible and hoping for more. Unbeknown to me, with that 'yes' God had gently planted within me the desire to live a wildly free and unbroken life. We were married when I was twenty, and spent the first years of our married life as a university couple, as Karl retrained to become an occupational therapist. He qualified just before our daughter was born three years later.

My next 'yes' moment happened a few months after Isabelle was born. Karl had successfully found a job in an almost unknown city in a rural county on the Welsh border. I was fighting fatigue and pain more than ever, and with a small child I was finding things really difficult. I had prayed many times before for healing, but had never received the relief I was seeking. I had lost hope that God would ever move on my behalf. Then one Sunday, as we sat at the back of our new church, with tears pouring down my face from the pain and despair, a gentle voice asked, 'Can I pray for you?' This was my next 'yes' moment. My heart did not believe it was possible, but my lips declared the word. 'Yes.'

God works powerfully when we say 'yes' to Him. When we give up our agendas and our timescales. In surrender and sometimes hopelessness our 'yes' can be turned into something that magnifies His glory. My small 'yes' led to a healed body and huge opportunity. Opportunity that included business, mission trips and adventure.

Fast forward twelve years and that life full of adventure had left us with a failed business, along with the debt that comes with it, and multiple house moves. But it had also grown between us a strong and vibrant marriage. We loved life, loved each other and loved our family. Our home was filled with more laughter than money, but the joy was worth it. And then came our next 'yes' opportunity. The failed business had left us unable to buy a house and permanent home for our daughter, but God challenged us to believe again. Did we believe that He could provide us with the deposit to buy a house? Failed businesses can steal hope for better things. God offered us a different choice. Do we say 'yes' again, or settle for a half measure life? In quiet confidence, we said it. I did believe that He could do it. I did not think He had to do it, but I knew He could. In multiple, miraculous ways, God provided the funds for our own family home.

And so this brings us to the latest 'yes' in our journey. This one has been far harder than all the rest. This 'yes' has required more trust than I ever thought I could have. It has taken me to hold on to joy most strongly and required me to fix my eyes on Jesus more firmly. Within three months of moving into our forever home, Karl found out that he had a brain tumour. These last few years have been a journey of learning to say 'yes' to Jesus daily, of coming before God broken and choosing to let Him rebuild me. Choosing to say yes daily. 'Yes', to trust, 'yes' to hope, 'yes' to joy. 'Yes' to Jesus.

This book is a compilation of my journey with God to thriving through this season. The chapters were each penned in or soon after pivotal moments He journeyed with me. I pray as we journey ahead they will bless you as much as they have grown me. The world will seek to break us to tame us. Jesus calls us to live an untamed life. A life lived wildly unbroken!

1. Pack your bags, Explorer

Welcome to your blessed life! I am so encouraged that you decided to take the time to open this book and take a peek. Inside these covers I hope you will discover the keys to living your blessed life. A life lived wild, free and full.

But before we begin, I need to set one thing straight. The day God placed this book in my heart I did not feel overly blessed. I had peeled open my eyes from sleep that morning and thumped my alarm clock into silence. Another day had arrived all too soon for my body. The clock was mercilessly making its way into another busy morning, with all the motherly things that needed doing before the school run and work started. I needed a holiday, but that was not looking likely. My husband, Karl, had undergone major brain surgery three months before, and it was looking like his return to work would not be happening any time soon. We were facing the daily struggles of work, school, life, and endless hospital appointments, all with an ever diminishing family budget. A holiday was the last thing we were likely to get.

Then, as ever the patient father, God spoke. His words rang clear and pure to my heart. My understanding of blessing and being blessed had become twisted up in a temporal and human understanding, and had lost the clear reflection of what He had designed it to be. I had bought into the lie that happiness and stuff meant blessing. This lie had sold me the pleasures of self as the eternal truth of heavenly blessing, and I had purchased it in bulk. That bleary eyed morning, God prompted my heart to start seeking the truth of what it means to live more than a blessed life but instead a truly wild and unbroken life full of

His blessings. He had started sifting my heart and shifting my thinking in search of His truth.

All journeys and adventures have a start point and a destination, and any journey worth making is taken by first consulting a map of some kind prior to setting out. So it is too when journeying life with God. We start with a question and expectantly await His response. With some questions God provides the answer quickly. But with other questions, the ones that really grow us and our faith, God has to take us on a quest through life and His Word to discover His answers. I believe that the quest for living the wildly unbroken life is one of those journeys. It is a journey full of heavenly diamonds ready to be unearthed with God. The broken world in which we live has tried to hide these truths from us, attempting to camouflage them amidst cheap imitations. An earthly snow used to obscure the truth and distract and confuse the heart. The challenge we face is seeing the diamonds where they are and not getting distracted with the cheaper glass imitations, or worse still, the worthless ice and snow. Our map book on this journey is the Bible. God's love letter and guidebook provided for His own.

This particular journey started in the early summer of 2017. Being in my mid thirties, I had been married to my first love for 15 years. We had full lives and were a happy family with a beautiful daughter. Both Karl and I were working for Christian organisations, had just bought our first home, and life was at last looking up. It had not been easy to get where we were. We had moved country, survived a failed business, conquered unemployment, and endured multiple house moves. We felt we had finally crossed our Jordan and were at long last living the blessed life in our very own land of milk and honey. What could possibly go wrong? We had God on our side, had ticked all the correct spiritual 'to' do boxes and were ready to live in what I perceived to be the blessings we had around us. But in the July of that year we received the news no one wants to hear.

When Karl was a very young child he had endured the horrors of brain cancer. As he had been treated successfully back then and was now mid forties, the whole ordeal was a distant memory. He had just undergone some routine tests due to the aches and pains of house moving, and what we assumed to be tension headaches, but was called back to his GP to discuss the results rather sooner than expected. They had found a tumour the size of a small orange growing on his brain. News like this rocks your world to the core. It can make you question your beliefs and leave you on your knees before God, asking 'why?' and begging Him for relief and healing.

The news ushered in our new adventure with God. This one was harder than any of the ones before, and one which we are still journeying through. I say this not to gain sympathy from you, but to gain equity with you, that our journey to this wildly unbroken life is one fought for not only in the pages of scripture, but also in the hard and dark valleys of life.

It started for me with a thought and question thrown up to God one morning. 'God, surely there is more to life than this?' When we ask this sort of question, we start to search for a deeper understanding of life. When this search leads us to the feet of Jesus we find there an awesome hope. This hope opens our heart to the vision that God has for us. One of living not only a blessed life, but a wildly unbroken life despite suffering or challenge. This wildly unbroken life we get to live needs searching for like a treasure, and hunted down.

Unlike earthly treasure, our treasure is hidden in plain sight. The world tries to hide it from view, but like diamonds hidden in snow that you cannot clearly see, our diamonds are revealed clear and sparkling when the heat comes and melts away the snow and ice. Sometimes the challenges and suffering we face are used by God to reveal His steadfast promises to us. The earthly distractions melt away in the heat of challenge but the heavenly diamonds don't. Diamonds are made in the hottest heat and under the greatest pressure, so they are fitting examples of the heavenly inheritance we have in Christ.

The beginning of the answer to my question snuck up on me unexpectedly one wet morning while on the school run. God sometimes does that. He waits for the place where you are least likely to expect the answer and He sneaks it in as a little surprise in your day. I was driving along an English country lane when I crossed a bridge over a river in flood. I had passed that way many times before and had always enjoyed the scene there. Trees along the picturesque bank, sheep in the nearby fields and of course the classic English countryside cottages. A picture of perfect countryside bliss. Today however the river had burst its banks and half submerged the trees in water. This was something I had witnessed before, but today the view had a depth I had not really seen before. The trees had withstood this flooding before and were still standing, growing, providing shelter and bearing fruit. God brought to my mind the words He gave to the prophet Jeremiah.[1]

But blessed is the one who trusts in the Lord,
whose confidence is in him.
They will be like a tree planted by the water
that sends out its roots by the stream.
It does not fear when heat comes;
its leaves are always green.
It has no worries in a year of drought
and never fails to bear fruit.

There was such strength in those words. Perhaps there was more to blessing and being blessed than I had first realised. There was something wild and unbroken in the trees that defied the destructive force of the water at their roots.

So began my journey to finding the truth in living the blessed life, and it is my pleasure to share it with you in the chapters ahead. I hope you will be inspired and encouraged as we delve deeper into God's Word, where I pray we will discover the diamonds He has placed for us in it. I believe God will reveal to us more than a few splinters of His precious rock, but rather great big gems of heavenly revelation. Gems big enough to alter the course of our lives and allow God to use us in ways far bigger than we could ever imagine. Ways far beyond our circumstances or limitations. This book is the product of an eventful and difficult few years of my life, where God held me so closely and guided me to the reality of living a fully blessed life, even though it looked like it was all falling apart. I pray that you too will be encouraged and inspired as you read, to journey with me to discovering your very own life lived wildly unbroken.

2. Base Camp

If I plan to go on a journey with a map, it is pretty important to ensure I know where I am before I can plot my course to where I am going. If I get my starting coordinates muddled, then my whole journey could go disastrously wrong. The same is true for God's Word and any journey we make through it. My spiritual perspective will have a huge impact on my journey of discovery with God and on my ultimate destination. It could either lead me to a heavenly treasure trove or to spiritual ruin. Before we set off together it is vital that we ensure that we set our internal spiritual compass to match up to God's Word. To do this, we need to explore a few questions together. I recommend that you take some time out with God to seek your own answers to these before we go on our journey. The preparation will be well worth it. We will periodically stop to pause as we journey together through this book to check our bearings. These moments are vital if we are to recalibrate our spiritual compasses to His Word before we proceed. I believe your honest reflections at these pause moments will give God greater and deeper opportunities to speak into and through your life. This will in turn spill out and impact your world.

The first question we need to ask ourselves in this journey of discovery is this, 'From where is our viewpoint of blessing grounded?' and following from that, 'Does this grounding line up with scripture?'

We all have an idea of what blessing is. Social media and advertising work together to suggest and reinforce the belief that it's all about the good stuff in life. It's all about the great house we get to live in, the popular fun loving friends we hang out with, or the latest fashion must haves we have just been able to purchase. I am sure most of us have seen the glossy social media posts complete with the hashtag #blessed. It's as though the proof of God's hand of favour and blessing on our lives is evidenced through the possession of these things. I suspect however, that there is a huge flaw in this thinking. Like two sides of a coin, if one side says that this is evidence of blessing, then the other side should say that the lack of the evidence of these things in our lives is the lack of blessing. This poses for me a big problem. If the nice stuff we have around us and our own physical comfort is evidence of blessing, does that, by reverse, mean that God has not blessed the passionate but persecuted Christians living in poverty, prison, or both in other parts of the world? Does it mean that having to meet together to study His Word in secret, or face imprisonment and torture, is proof of a lack of blessing?

I have faced many times in my life where I have lived through terrible, physical or emotional pain.

Did that mean that at those points in my life God had removed His blessing from me and left me to fend for myself? This does not match up with what we read in Jeremiah 15:7 where it says,

But blessed is the one who trusts in the Lord,
whose confidence is in him.

I don't think I could ever seriously consider saying that the passionate but persecuted church around the world, both past and present, have not put their trust and confidence in the Lord. I have also found that it has been in my times of deepest hurt and pain where I have more earnestly reached out to my Father God. It is in those moments where I have placed my trust, hope and confidence in Him more than at any other time.

This leaves us facing a dilemma. I know that I serve a gracious and generous God who wants to give good gifts to His children. But if the idea that material possessions and physical comfort equals blessing has not matched up to my experience of living a life of faith, or the experiences of the persecuted church around the world, then has our viewpoint of blessing been misaligned? And if our viewpoint of blessing is misaligned, then our journey's start point is not centred correctly on God's Word. And if our start point is wrong, then we need to dig deeper in God's Word for truth before we continue.

So what is blessing? Perhaps what we have understood to be a blessing is instead a life of privilege? While I fully believe at the point of writing this that there is nothing wrong with privilege, I also hold that it can cloud and blinker our perspective of God. Our God lives outside of our narrow mindsets and understanding. He has a far bigger, clearer and three dimensional perspective of our lives and world than we do, and He wants us to experience more of that too. While happiness and physical comfort are wonderful, and parts of life for which I am extremely grateful, it is in the valleys of struggle and pain that we are given the opportunities to experience and share His love and joy at its deepest and fullest. The joy I speak of is not some warm fuzzy feeling that disappears as soon as it has made its appearance, but the quiet depth of understanding that He is good despite what I can see or feel. I experienced that joy while sitting for 8 hours waiting for Karl to come out of brain surgery. Not knowing whether he would walk, talk or even know me when he woke up. Not knowing if he would wake up. The joy that filled me that day was not one that had me dancing up the hospital corridors, instead it gave me the peace to know that no matter what, God had not left us alone. He was just as much with us in the operating theatre and intensive care unit as He was with us on our wedding day.

The truth is that God is eternal. He lives outside of time and space and yet comes to join us within the confines of it. He is the maker and giver of happiness, physical comfort, joy and blessing. Happiness and physical comfort are founded in the mortal and temporal confines of our world. Joy and blessing, however, are grounded and fuelled in the storehouses of the heavenly courts. They are eternal cords that pierce the temporal boundaries of time and space, drawing us closer to our heavenly father and calling us ever homewards to Him.

To more fully understand blessing, we need to go back to the beginning and the original blessing that God gave mankind at the start of creation. Genesis 1:27-28 says,

So God created mankind in his own image,
in the image of God he created them;
male and female he created them.
God blessed them and said to them, "Be fruitful
and increase in number; fill the earth and
subdue it. Rule over the fish in the sea and the
birds in the sky and over every living creature
that moves on the ground."

God repeats this blessing again to Noah and his sons after the great flood in Genesis 9:1,

Then God blessed Noah and his sons, saying to them, "Be fruitful and increase in number and fill the earth."

In both cases an instruction followed the blessing. God gave blessing not out of self merit or reward, but as an act of His love for mankind. There was an action that God desired in response to this blessing; He commissioned mankind to be fruitful and multiply, and to fill the earth.

A few generations on from Noah we see a new character emerge from God's Word and Abram comes onto the scene. God made Abram an enormous promise. He promised Abram that He would give him more descendants than the dust on the earth[1] or stars in the sky,[2] and that through him the whole earth would be blessed.

The Lord had said to Abram, "Go from your country, your people and your father's household to the land I will show you.

"I will make you into a great nation, and I will bless you;

I will make your name great,
and you will be a blessing.
I will bless those who bless you,
and whoever curses you I will curse;
and all peoples on earth
will be blessed through you."[3]

God told Abram that he would be blessed and that he would be a blessing to others. Again, there is an action desired in response to the blessing, not to gain, it but because of it.

Abram goes on the journey with God, trusting His promise of blessing. He receives a new name, Abraham, and is given the family he never thought possible. God repeats this action of blessing and fruitfulness in Abraham's descendants, Isaac, Jacob, Joseph and then to Ephraim and Manasseh. They were all given this same blessing.

We find Abraham and his descendants in the lineage of Christ.[4] And it is in Christ that promise of blessing the world through him came into fullness.[5]

In all this we need to understand that if we already have blessing through the completed work of Christ on the cross, and it is as a response to this gift that we live a fruitful life, then we can do nothing extra to earn it.[6]

Too many times I have read and heard of occasions where we are told that we need to do, give, go… and then God will bless us. While I fully believe that God does reward the generous heart when it is focused on Him, this 'give to get' blessing mentality can lead us to believe that we have to earn favour with God. It can even lead us to think it is possible to buy God's favour, as if He is some genie god, that if we do the right things He has to bless us.

It can put us in a place where we begin bargaining with God and hold Him to a contract He never signed. Then when things don't work out the way we wanted them to, we blame God for breaking His side of the agreement. God, however, never bought in to that agreement.

Scripture says that the earth is the Lord's and everything in it.[7] So why would we think something we can do would buy God's favour and blessing, when He already owns the cattle on a thousand hills,[8] and anything we could give Him He already owns?

This point gains extra weight when we see that God's promise of blessing made to Abraham was given to him approximately 430 years before God gave the Law to Moses. Galatians 3:17 shows us that the promise of blessing superseded the Law, and was made in response to the relationship God had with Abraham.

> *What I mean is this: the law, introduced 430 years later, does not set aside the covenant previously established by God and thus do away with the promise.*

It was something God did for Abraham, rather than because of something Abraham did for God. It was a promise made to Abraham through an active relationship with God.

This leads us neatly to the next point. If blessing is not something we can earn, and there was a right response of fruitfulness to blessing at the start, then surely there is a right response to blessing we have now. Blessing was never intended to be kept for ourselves, but to be met with an outpouring of ourselves into the world. Christ was the ultimate example of this principle, where He poured himself out for our benefit. While we were still lost and broken in sin He came for us.[9]

God loves people. He continually gave the command to His people to increase and multiply, and to fill the earth. The Great Commission Jesus gave His disciples[10] after His resurrection was to go out into all the earth and make disciples.

God never intended heaven to be empty of people. He wanted it filled with His children. A people who would love Him back as He loved us first. But the love He desires is one designed in free will and choice rather, than a forced obligation. The Old Testament people of God were instructed to fill the earth: the New Testament people of God are now instructed to fill heaven.

Galatians 3:29 says,

> *If you belong to Christ, then you are Abraham's seed, and heirs according to the promise.*

And again in Galatians 4:28 it says,

> *Now you, brothers and sisters, like Isaac, are children of promise.*

If we take Abraham's promise of blessing as being fulfilled through Christ's life, death and resurrection, then we need to take one more step. If through Christ the whole earth is blessed, then adding this truth to what we read in Jeremiah 15:7 about blessing being based on our trust and confidence in God, then as His followers we inherit this promise as our own. Blessing becomes something not to be obtained, but something we already have.

We are already blessed! There is no formula for blessing other than being united with Christ, and this is something we cannot earn.

If we are already blessed, and blessing is not about stuff and physical comfort, then how do we live in this blessing, especially when living through the hard times of pain or suffering?

Like Abraham, we need to go on our own adventure, leaving our old nature, understanding and biases behind, and head out into the journey of discovering the fullness of living the blessed life with God. Leaving base camp behind, and with our compass correctly set, I think we are ready to head out onto the mountain for the climb to the summit.

Check Your Bearings

- ○ Blessing is not something to be obtained, but something we already have.
- ○ This blessings is not for us to keep for ourselves, but something to pass on to those around us.

3. The Climb

In the last chapter we discovered that blessing is something we already have, not something to obtain, and we see that our response to blessing is to pour that out into the world around us. But how do we do this at those times in our lives when it feels like it's all falling apart?

I will bring you back to my experiences of living the wildly unbroken life. The day I started to pen this chapter, I can honestly say that I felt conflicted. I would love to say this revelation of being blessed was framed with a bright and sunny British summer day, complete with picnics in the sun and strawberries with cream. What I must say instead is that I was sitting alone with Jesus. It was a cold room on a murky day, and the rain was thumping down on the windows. The bank balance was ever diminishing, and the recent hospital visits had told us we faced more treatments and investigations. Karl's health was getting worse, and my ability to work the hours I needed was looking increasingly difficult.

And yet God's Word said that despite all of that, I was living in His blessing. I was and still am blessed. They were hard words to swallow when it looked so bleak. So what does blessing look like when in situations like these?

How about we get that map out from Chapter 1 and get going on our adventure of discovery? We have left base camp and started to climb the mountain ahead. Chapter 2 got our compass bearings straight, so I hope by the end of this expedition we will have reached His summit of revelation, and picked up more of His precious gems.

With all ascents there is a climb, and climbing can be painful. It's the time when we really wrestle with God. When we test every step we take, making sure our feet are planted firmly before the next step is taken. It can be a slow and scary progress. One that grows our strength, tests our trust and stretches our endurance.

I recently went on a walk up a hill local to me with some ladies from our church. The first part of the journey was filled with the general chatter that ladies do. Laughter and jokes. Sharing the joys and challenges of raising children, working, building businesses and running homes. Some of us stepped up the pace, wanting to prove to ourselves that we could reach the summit first. The female competitive spirit is a powerful force. I found, however, that I was not as fit as I first thought. The flat foot of the hill was now behind us, and we had started to ascend the slope to the top. This hill was not overly high or steep, but I was very soon out of breath. My pride and determination did not want to stop for a rest. I was determined to get to that summit and not be seen to be weak or unfit.

However, the further I went the more out of breath I got. My lungs burned as I breathed, and my muscles ached. I could hear and feel my heart thump loudly in my ears. Chatting, laughing, or even talking no longer interested me. I just wanted to get to the top of that hill. I was looking for anything to help me keep going. Tree trunks became supports to help pull my next step in front of me. Roots and rocks became footholds. Thirst was yelling at my throat, but I did not want to stop for fear that my legs would refuse to get going again if I did.

And in this part of the climb the atmosphere of the group started to change. Ladies started using their words to spur each other on in encouragement. Water bottles were given to those who needed a drink. The fit helped the less fit, and the competition gave way to becoming a group effort. It was no longer a case of who gets there first wins, but let no-one be left behind. The view at the top was stunning and the triumph for all was powerful. We needed each other unified to reach the summit.

How similar is this to the times in life when the going gets tough. It's tempting to let pride take over, and say that we are doing just fine. To hide any form of weakness in case we get called out as some lesser form of human, or, heaven forbid, prove to others that our Christian exterior is not as perfect as we hope it looks to others. After all, is it not right that Christians should be all together and perfect in times of difficulty? Or perhaps just being a Christian means that tough stuff does not happen to us? Like being expected to climb the hill with a full face of makeup and not breaking into a sweat.

I think we are all agreed that that last statement is untrue. The Bible is full of words of encouragement for those of us going through times of real trial and difficulty. Our faith does not exempt us from the trials of life, but it gives us hope in the midst of them. This hope is like the water and rest we need to help sustain us while we walk through them. It gives us the strength to endure through both trails and suffering. Psalm 42:1-2a puts it beautifully;

As the deer pants for streams of water,

so my soul pants for you, my God.

My soul thirsts for God, for the living God.

In the midst of difficulties it only takes one person to start to change the focus for those around them. Like our hill walk, it took one person to see that one other person who needed a word or two of encouragement to spur them on. And once one person starts, it becomes a contagious force. We have within us the source of rest and water that can fuel and encourage others in times of difficulty. We have our faith in Jesus! When we see others on their tough journey, alone and without the hope we have in Christ, we have a choice to make. We can either leave them to struggle on alone, or we can take the opportunity we have been given to stop and offer them the life giving water and rest available through Christ.

Furthermore, we have the equity of a genuine and heartfelt understanding of their journey. One fuelled by His love and compassion and ignited by faith. We become living vessels positioned by God to pour out His refreshing hope and strength to those around us. Surely that is blessing?

Climbing is a pursuit that should never be undertaken alone. If you are facing a difficult situation right now, I encourage you to stop here for a moment, and before continuing ask yourself this question. Who is my climbing buddy? Who will help hold me up when things are tough and I am tired? And to whom can I come alongside and do the same?

If we look back at the creation story in Genesis 2, we find the story of Adam and Eve. It starts with God placing Adam in the Garden of Eden, a perfect paradise for him to live in and to enjoy. God designed the garden specifically for Adam to tend, nurture and commune with him. However, in the midst of this perfection God says,

It is not good for the man to be alone.[1]

In the perfection of the garden, without trials and difficulties, God understood that Adam needed companionship in the work of tending it. So why then, when we adventure life with God, which is full of twists, turns, danger, and difficulty rather than perfection, do we think that we should suck it all in and manage on our own? We were never called to do this life alone, and your climbing buddy is as essential to your journey as you are to theirs.

This is not an idea found only in the opening chapters of Genesis. All through scripture there are stories of Bible heroes who buddied up. Moses had Aaron, Naomi had Ruth, Jonathan had his armour bearer, David had his mighty men, and Elijah had Elisha. In each case there were crises or dangerous situations to be faced, and our heroes could not have carried out their God given journeys without their climbing buddies.

Yes, you read that right. Their journeys were God-given. Moses' journey included a murderous past before breaking a nation out of slavery. Naomi's journey to being the multiple great grandmother of Jesus included facing widowhood, losing her only sons and providing for her widowed daughters-in-law. By far my favourite duo in this season is Jonathan and his armour bearer. You can read their story in 1 Samuel 14:1-13, where you find the people of Israel being oppressed by the Philistine army. Jonathan, King Saul's son, had just about had enough of the oppression. He sought God's permission, then took the brave steps to break free from his place of containment. Together with his armour bearer they stepped out of the shadows and fought their oppressors. God, who had agreed to their request, went before them into their battle, and sealed their victory. Their victory had been assured by God, but it still took a precarious climb to obtain it. Together they scaled the steep rock face, having to use both their hands and their feet for the climb. Together they climbed, together they fought and together they received their victory. Jonathan needed his climbing buddy on that day.

I have learned through the various climbing seasons of my life that it is OK to question God in difficult situations. If you never question God, then you miss out on opportunities for God to grow your faith. If you did not check your ropes and harnesses before a climb, would you trust that they could hold you while hanging from a ledge? Jonathan sought God's agreement before he started the hill climb to battle and victory. Questioning God is how we check our spiritual ropes and harnesses. It is not a matter of testing God because you believe Him to be unfaithful, but knowing your God-given equipment, so that despite your difficulties you are certain of His goodness. Our faith is a gift. It is equipment we are to get to know how to use daily, but is most valued while on a climb and not left in the toolbox.

Check your bearings

○ Hope is the refreshing water and rest we need while we journey the tough chapters of life.

○ Challenge gives us the opportunity to be living vessels, positioned by God to pour out His refreshing hope and strength to those around us.

○ We were never called to do life alone: who is your climbing buddy?

4. It's Getting Dark Out Here!

Hills can be climbed in an afternoon. Some larger ones may take a day. But real mountains are not a day trip. They are expedition adventures, where you are called to travel through the wild for days, weeks or even months. To sleep under canvas or even the stars.

Our journey to living wildly unbroken is an expedition and not a day trip. When you go on an expedition, you don't expect to be home, warm and dry by night fall. You may hope for comfort, but nothing is certain. The adventurer should be prepared to sleep out in the wild, with the stars and moon for company.

So far on our journey, we have explored our map, ropes, harnesses and climbing gear. We have also discovered the importance of having a climbing buddy to walk alongside us on our journey.

In the next few chapters we will explore the night season in our journey. We will examine the possible dangers we may face in them, and discover the tools we need to overcome these with God. The tools we get in the next three chapters may shape us far more than the daylight seasons of our journey, and equip us with the skills that we need for the rest of our expedition deeper into living the wildly unbroken life.

There is a profound truth to be found in the way God made mankind. We were created to be diurnal. To be diurnal means to be awake during the day and asleep at night. We were designed to work and create during the daytime. To build and grow in the light of God's goodness, and to rest and sleep in His comfort and presence at night.

Because of our diurnal nature, we have a greater understanding of what can be seen. In our broken world, the challenges of daytime are very real and visible. This makes us more confident to rationalise and plan, when we understand the problems and challenges that we face. Daylight helps limit the power that we can allow fear to have over us.

In the same way, the challenges of night are very different to those faced in the daylight. Even the creatures who roam the wild at night look very different to those of daytime. Night time does strange things to our human state. Our senses become heightened and our imaginations go into overdrive. A creak or squeak heard in daylight is ignored, but at night it is given priority focus. Shadows that in the clear light of day may seem innocent become menacing, and are given the potential to be something both dangerous and terrifying. The neighbour's dog that wanders down the garden path in the daytime for a game of ball suddenly becomes a deadly predator, ready to pounce and kill. In the dark we can be tempted to give focus to the voices of uncertainty and fear.

The night in our adventure is an uncertain time of waiting. A time where we cannot go forward into what is next, but we cannot go backwards either. We have to wait for the night to pass, trusting in the One who flung the stars into place and believing He knows what the dawn brings, whether it be a battle or not.

The season of night time waiting is one where we have to actively participate in learning to rest in His peace. Where we need to grow a deeper trust in Him despite the 'what if?' questions that keep coming to rob us of our peace.

Psalm 3:5-6 reassures us as follows;

I lie down and sleep;
I wake again, because the Lord sustains me.
I will not fear though tens of thousands

assail me on every side.

Here we are encouraged not to fear the night or the battle. It does not say that the battle does not come, but it does reassure us that He is fighting for us in it. That reassurance is given to help us to rest in His presence in the midst of the battle.

When camping in the wilderness we take it in turns to be on night watch. Someone is tasked with keeping the campfire burning and being on watch to raise the alarm in case of danger or attack. We have the beautiful assurance from our God that He is our watchman in the night times of our lives.

I lift up my eyes to the mountains –
where does my help come from?
My help comes from the Lord,
the Maker of heaven and earth.
He will not let your foot slip –
he who watches over you will not slumber;
indeed, he who watches over Israel
will neither slumber nor sleep.

The Lord watches over you –
the Lord is your shade at your right hand;
the sun will not harm you by day,
nor the moon by night.
The Lord will keep you from all harm –
he will watch over your life;
the Lord will watch over your coming and going
both now and for evermore.[1]

The challenge we face is that instead of fearing the battle or the danger, we need to trust that He is big enough to fight on our behalf. While He is fighting on our behalf, we need to rest in His presence and wait for the night time to pass.

For some of us this uncertain night time season of trusting is longer than it is for others. The dark in those times can feel so overwhelming that it is almost able to be touched, like a thick blanket that you cannot remove from in front of your face. My night time waiting season lasted for two years. Two years of medical tests, uncertainty of the future, and the inability to make plans. Two years of waiting for Karl's diagnoses and prognoses. We waited without knowing whether the symptoms we faced were permanent or temporary. If we had known the answers to those questions we would have been able to plan our future and our finances. Instead we had to sit it out in the dark and learn to rest in His presence without fearing for the future.

The night time waiting and uncertainty I felt during those two years of waiting could have been likened to waiting in the dark of the predawn before a battle in the days of old. Those days when hand to hand combat was how battles were fought and won. Where you faced your foe, eye to eye, weapon to weapon, and you could hear their cries and taunts.

You could not do anything before light was shed on the battlefield, so you waited in the dark for the daylight to come. You would try your best to be strong and calm, but would become ever aware of the noises of the battle lines in opposition to you. You could hear the clinking of their weapons and the shuffle and stamping of their feet in the cold. You wouldn't know how many warriors were before you. You didn't even know how battle hardened or experienced they were. All you knew was what you could hear. Whispers, clinking, stamping and your own heart beating in your chest. All you could do was be still and wait for the sunrise. Be careful of the fearful half whispers and noises of the dark seasons. They do not seek you out to bring you peace. The prophet Isaiah reminds us that our peace and confidence is only found in God.

So do not fear, for I am with you;
do not be dismayed, for I am your God.
I will strengthen you and help you;
I will uphold you with my righteous right hand[2]

There is a danger in this campsite season too. It can be easy to stop in the place of temporary camping and stay there. We can become accustomed to the fearful noises and uncertainty. Almost so comfortable with hearing the unknown that it becomes our new normal and familiar. We are tempted to believe that there will never be daytime, so we should stop trusting in God. We can begin to blinker our eyes away from the hope of the horizon where dawn appears. Despair and bitterness can start to take root. Bitterness steals hope and joy and binds us in the shackles of dark cynicism. Cynicism tells us that we are abandoned by God in the dark. We can begin to refuse to journey on through the season of trust and rest, and instead make our new home in the uncertain darkness. It can be surprisingly easy in times like this to be of the attitude that it is better to live with the challenge and difficulty I know than face a new one.

When facing the whispers in the dark it is vitally important that you speak out the words of hope left for you in the Bible. When you are tempted to stop trusting, remind yourself of God's faithfulness;

Your love, Lord, reaches to the heavens, your faithfulness to the skies.[3]

When you are tempted to believe that you are abandoned by God, remember the words of Moses to Joshua;

> *Be strong and courageous. Do not be afraid or terrified because of them, for the Lord your God goes with you; he will never leave you nor forsake you.*[4]

The greatest weapon we have against bitterness is a thankful heart. Every day find one thing to be thankful for. The more we seek these things out the easier it becomes. Thankfulness will help keep our hearts soft and is a powerful antidote to bitterness.

Expeditions are not places of settlement. God calls us to go deeper in Him, to understand His superiority in greater depth, and own our inheritance with greater confidence. The adventurer's campsite was never meant to be a place to settle. The morning will come, and when it comes we need to be ready to pack up and move on.

In this chapter we have started to look at the waiting season in our journey to the blessed life. We have discovered how it is a season of actively growing trust while we rest in His presence and peace. We have also looked at how we can become accustomed to this place and be tempted to settle here, rather than move on to a greater degree of trust in God, in order to step into the next part of our adventure.

Now is a great time to write a list of thanks for the things He has provided in this night season of waiting. We will come back to this list in the coming chapters, so take your time to do this. It will also help to put your thanks list up somewhere that you can regularly see it. Seeing your list in the hard days will help you to remain thankful and trusting that He has you firmly in His hands, even if you feel alone and all around you is dark.

Check your bearings

○ Take some time out with God to rest in His presence and peace.

○ Look back at how far you have come and how He has never let you down.

○ Thankfulness is a great counter to the dangers of cynicism and bitterness that have faced us down in this season.

5. Night Time

I have learned through my journey that the night time is also the time where we have to learn to grieve. It seems a strange thing to say that grief is something you learn to do, but just as you learn to walk as a toddler, we need to learn to grieve as adults. This is not a morbid grief where we sit it out in despair. We have a real hope in Christ, so any despair we could have had, Christ has taken.

Our journey to the wildly unbroken life in challenge has included losing elements of our old life. While some of our old life was bad, some of it may have been pretty good too! But the place of blessing is a place of even better. So we need to move into that place. When we move into that place of even better, it can be a painful process, where God strips away from us the things that were holding us back from His next best for us. The place of heavenly blessing is a place of selfless and pure love. First received from God and then poured out to those around us. But we, as vessels before God, sometimes need to be emptied first in order to be filled with the purity of who He is. A dirty vessel cannot hold clean water and keep the water clean. God first washes the dirt from our lives and then fills us with the purity of Him. This stripping back can be the most painful part of our journey, and sometimes it happens in the dark places, where we cannot see what He is doing. The washing and cleaning process of the Holy Spirit can be a painful experience. In this process we need to remind ourselves that God wastes nothing of our experiences, and He can and will use the suffering season of our lives to renew us into more of the likeness of His son.

We know that in all things God works for the good of those who love him, who have been called according to his purpose.[1]

When we don't know what the future holds it is easy to hold on to the past all the more firmly. God, however, asks us to let go of the past in order to step into the future. This letting go is not meant to be a meaningless throwing away, however. It is a place of intentionally and purposefully putting things down. If we lose things we never intended to put down, we always carry within us a grief and loss for that which was. When we purposefully thank God for the past we have had and purposefully hand it over to Him, we relinquish the rights to that past. It allows us to walk free into the future with the good memories of what it was, but with hope for what will be. That is the purpose of this part of our night time.

It is time alone with God, where we thank Him for what was, and bit by bit hand it over to Him. This is not something you have to rush. It is better to take your time truly thanking Him for the past, remembering it with Him, and then handing it over to Him. The rights to that past are given to Him in exchange for a fuller, more beautiful future. We let go of all bitterness that may come from holding on to the past.

We need to learn to grieve the past, and the things that were, to be free to worship God in the new place of freedom. This is something the Israelites never fully learned to do in their desert wanderings. It was always a case of looking back and wishing that they had what they used to have. Blaming Moses or God for what they had lost, rather than expectantly looking forward to the fruitful future God had promised.

When we learn to grieve and then release, we find that we are truly free to praise God in the dessert places. We get to leave the past with its hurt and joy with God, and stand in the lightness and freedom He has for us.

Even Jesus grieved. We read in Luke how He grieved for Jerusalem and its rebellion.[2] We also read in John 11 how He grieved for His good friend Lazarus.[3] He allowed himself to go to that place of feeling the pain of loss. The difference between the grief of Jerusalem and the grief of Lazarus was that when Jesus called Lazarus from the tomb, He emerged from it, even though still covered in the grave clothes, and stepped into the second chance of life that Christ offered. Jerusalem however, turned their back on Him instead. What could have been a city that welcomed its maker and king, instead rejected the life He was offering it. We have a choice in our places of grief too. We can 'go there,' feeling the pain of the loss and bearing the hopes of what could have been, and stay there. Or step out of that place, and then call out of the death and pain the newness of life that Jesus has for us. Lazarus's story could have been just another one of the 'Jesus healed me' stories. Instead, he got to be part of an even greater miracle. A 'Jesus brought me back to life' kind of a miracle.

In our grief there is an opportunity to call some life back into our story. This life may look totally different from any life we have already experienced. I believe in my heart that it should look totally different from that which was before. And the reason it should look different is because our life beyond the place of grief is lived from the perspective of having seen the darkest places of our soul, and then been freed to walk out the other side.

Jesus said,

> *Blessed are those who mourn, for they will be comforted.*[4]

It is in the mourning and grief that the comfort comes. Not on the other side of it, as though we need to strive through it. The blessing is given in the midst of the pain, while it still hurts! But in order for us to pass the comfort to others while still in our pain.

I remember well the day I sat in my garden feeling those feelings of grief. I was surrounded by DIY jobs, as well as the day to day chores that life throws at us. But I stopped for a bit and took a few moments out with God, and let myself go to the place of 'what if...?'

What if Karl had not had the brain tumours? What if he had still had the tumours, but the surgery and recovery had been an overwhelming success, and he was totally well? What if he was still working full time, and we had the life everyone else seemed to have...?

I let myself 'go there' and feel the pain of the loss. But instead of letting the pain build up inside me, I poured it out to God. And in that place of emptying myself of all the pain, while still allowing myself to feel every bit of it, He reminded me of some aspects of our journey. These aspects were called relationships. They had the names of real people and dear friends.

If Karl was fully well, then our lives would not be filled with the precious people this journey has brought into our lives. Some of these people started out as those therapy workers tasked to help Karl get better, but have now become dearly loved friends. In a blink, 'my what?' if had erased them from our lives. Then the tears really came. I could not imagine our lives without these precious friends. Not because of what they invested into us, but because of the potential we saw in them, that we know only God can release.

So what does life look like beyond the grave clothes of grief? When we are stripped back of all we were, and are wrapped in the grave clothes of loss and grief, Jesus starts to call us out again. And when He calls us out from our dark place, He removes the last remnants of the grave clothes from us and starts to reclothe us with His God-given identity. We have a fullness of understanding, compassion and love we had not experienced before our time in the dark.

This season of stripping back and reclothing is key to us entering our new season of fruitfulness. Remember we are already blessed, and through that blessing we are called to fruitfulness. Remember how Jeremiah reminded us that those who trust in the Lord are like trees that bear fruit, regardless of the drought or rain.[5]

Every new part of our journey to the wildly unbroken life cannot be entered into while still holding on to yesterday's fruit. As we leave night time and head into dawn, the fruitfulness we are entering is a different, fuller and deeper fruitfulness than the one we had at the start of our journey. It is called maturity.

You see this fruitfulness shift in nature. The evidence of the life in a spring plant is in its flowers. You could perhaps say that the fruitfulness of the spring plant is seen in its flowers. However, the flower's petals must fall for the flower to become fruit, and the autumn fruit must fall for the future seed to be set free.

Likewise my fruitfulness depends upon a stripping back in order to unleash the seeds of heavenly fruitfulness.

We live in a world where youth is valued and beauty is considered to be a thing for the young. This twisted understanding of beauty has gone deep into the heart of the western church too. We have lost our ability to see the fruitful beauty in the stripped-back seasons of life. We have focused so much on the beauty of the rose bud that we have lost our ability to see the beauty and value in the rose hip. However, this stripping back needs to happen to release fruitfulness. If I hold onto my 'now' season, it restricts the release of my next season. A closed flower cannot make and release seed. If the seed is not released then the reproduction of the plant is restricted. My unwillingness to let go will influence the impact my life will have on others. The influence I have will be one of rotting, or of life. Holding on leads to bitter stagnation. Letting go leads to fresh life.

Are we willing to grieve and then let go of what was, in order to step into what God has next? Perhaps take some time now with God to thank Him for what was, and let Him strip back your grave clothes, so you can enter into the next part of your journey without tripping over the remnants of your last one.

Also take some time to thank God for the people and relationships He has strategically placed in your journey. They are not a mistake, and will form a deeper part of living your wildly unbroken life than you may realise now.

Check your bearings

- When we learn to grieve and then release, we find that we are truly free to praise God in the desert places.
- Maturity and fruitfulness come from letting go of one season, so you can step into the next one.

○   It is important to thank God for the people and relationships He has strategically placed in your journey. They are not a mistake and will form a deeper part of living your blessed life than you may realise.

6. Sunrise is Coming

When a new day starts to dawn, an eerie silence takes hold of nature. The sounds that filled the dark and tried to scare us while night took hold, quieten down, leaving an empty in between silence. The silence where the noises of night stop, but sounds of the new day have yet to start. The dawn chorus of the birds is yet to begin and the sun has not yet poked its rays above the horizon. As the temperature drops, we can be forgiven for thinking that a deeper and lonelier night has taken hold, rather than believing that we sit on the brink of a new day.

It is in this eerie silence that we take the first steps into our true identity in Christ. Loss can leave you empty and forgetting who you are. As you process this loss and work through the grief, it is important to allow God to fill you up with more of who He is. This is the point where you start the journey of rediscovering who you are. Not what you had or did in the past, but who He made you to be.

No-one but Jesus can reveal to you your true identity. It is not something that your pastor, spouse, or best friend can tell you. It is also not something that family members can enforce on you. Fashion will say that you can reinvent yourself every season. Technology can tell you that you can hide behind a fake or photoshopped picture on social media. But these are only superficial and broken coverings for the searching heart. Our godly friends and leaders can advise us of what the scriptures say about our identity, but only Christ can truly reveal to you who you are. It is something that has to happen deep inside you before it can manifest itself on the outside in fullness. Lazarus stepped out of the tomb, not to the sound of his sisters' calls or his friends' cries, but at the call of Jesus. Jesus then released Him from the bondage of his grave clothes. Lazarus would have had to be dressed in new clothes once the grave clothes were removed.

Jesus has new clothes for you too. The night time season was where the old clothes were removed. The dawn is where your new clothes and identity are revealed to you. Who you truly are is something that Jesus wants to speak into the depth of your heart in the quiet places of your dawn season, where you are totally alone with Him. There is no noise and chatter from others as to what you should be doing, saying, or looking like. It is simply you and Jesus. It is a beautiful place of quiet surrender. A precious and vulnerable place where His gentleness works wonders with your life. It is also the safest place you can ever be.

This place of quiet silence is the starting position of the journey to your God-given identity. Walking in His fullness and blessing is not something that can be done in its fullest and richest when you don't really know who you are. When you understand your position as His dearly loved child, you start to more fully understand your inherited position in Him .

The Bible reminds us that through Christ you are a holy priest, set apart for His service.[1] You are no longer a slave to this world, but hold a position of authority in the heavenly places under God.[2] He had dressed you in new clothes of heavenly holiness.

We can see examples of this when we look at the making of the tabernacle in Exodus. It was built from the inside to the outside, and I believe that is what God does with us. He renews us from the inside first, then dresses the outside. The glorious brilliance of who He is, and His presence then shines through to the outside of us. It is something that fancy makeup and designer clothing cannot do for your body. It is a holy exchange of your brokenness for His wholeness. Our mess for His beauty. Our lives for His life.

My own personal experience of the start of this dawn season came as a total surprise to me. I realised while walking through the grief of all we had lost as a family, that I no longer knew who I was. In the stripping back, God had beautifully revealed to me that my understanding of who I was had been formulated from the place of what I was good at, or what was useful to others, rather than the qualities He had placed deep within me that caused my heart to leap for joy, and made me uniquely different from anyone else. I sat one day in the middle of the piles of laundry and half washed dishes, and realised that I no longer knew what I liked or not. I had gone to the place of serving and loving my family so deeply that I no longer even knew if I liked spaghetti, or the colour pink. This could have caused me distress. However, because of the work God had done in me by stripping me back, and the deep love I have for my family, I suddenly saw the beauty of the adventure that was before me.

God was inviting me onto the next part of my journey with Him. And this journey was one of discovering who He made me to be. It was the opportunity to try new things without fear of whether I liked them, or of the opinions of others. What mattered most to me was God's opinion of me, and that His opinion should be all that mattered. His opinion and love for me was to be the frame around the mirror of my own self evaluation.

If I switch this round and place my own self evaluation as the frame for how I perceive God to value and love me, then I am on dodgy ground. It means that when I am having a bad day, and who doesn't get those, I can believe that God thinks less of me that day. Or on those days when pride comes knocking and I give in to self righteousness, because we all fall short here too, I can end up devaluing others.

However, when I get the frame right it shifts my perspective off myself and onto God and who He says I am. This shifted focus allows me to see that my position as His dearly loved daughter goes ahead of whether I am having a good day, or what others think of me. Your reframed focus will help form your stepping into the new day, and the song you get to sing as you step into it.

How about we take this value principle a step further? Imagine being in a house that is not your home. This home belongs to a good friend of yours, and you are visiting for the weekend. Would you help yourself to the contents of their fridge? What would be your level of influence in deciding on whether the living room needed to be redecorated, or if the kitchen cupboards needed to be reorganised? I have some great friends, but there are some things I would not consider doing or having a say over in their home in the same way as I would in my own home.

If I were in my parents' home for the weekend however, I would be more likely to have access to, or influence over situations to a greater degree than at my friends' homes. The point to this illustration is the importance of understanding our identity and position in Christ as we see the sunrise of our new day. We have the rights of sons and daughters of the King of Heaven.

When we give our lives to Christ, we let go of the rights to do whatever we want with our lives, and give Him the authority to lead us. We start to play by His rules. But these rules are adhered to as sons and daughters of God, rather than as a guest of the house. The rules are set by God, but we have a level of authority and influence in the house. When we are purely unrelated guests, we still live by the rules of that house, but hold no authority or influence to affect change.

Our new life found in Christ gives us the authority to evict from our lives any parts that are not compatible with the decor of heavenly holiness. Take a few moments and ask yourself this question. Are there areas of your life where you have become comfortable with the mismatched decor? Perhaps this is because you have felt that you have no say in changing it. If you have no say in changing the decor, then you may as well get used to it. This mismatched decor could be as simple as an attitude you felt you couldn't change, or the crippling grip of fear that stops you trying something new. It could be the attitude of cynicism, or fear that you will never have enough money to support your family. Or perhaps you struggle with confidence, and the thought of meeting new people is overwhelming.

Our new identity in Christ opens our eyes to the reality of our position as sons and daughters in His house. We have authority to make these changes in our lives. In fact Jesus wants us to take some authority in these parts of our lives. He has given us the authority.

Scripture says that we are now co-heirs with Christ.[3] A co-heir is not a servant, but a leader of the house. You have God-given authority to step up and take ownership of that which Christ has bought for you. He has not just set you free from sin, but has bought you freedom. Being set free is one thing. Being bought your freedom and given an inheritance is another. One comes only with release from oppression, while the other comes with release of resources and authority.

The whole earth is filled with awe at your wonders;
where morning dawns, where evening fades,
you call forth songs of joy.[4]

As the sun begins to rise on our lives, the coldness passes away and the birds start to sing once more. Their song heralds the dawn chorus of new beginnings. This dawn chorus can sound like a cacophony of chaos compared to the deathly quiet and stillness of predawn moments. But if you take time to listen carefully, you can make out individual types of birdsong. In your new morning, when God clothes you in your new identity as His co-heir in the kingdom, He gives you a new song to sing in your new morning. You are released from singing exactly like everyone else, and are finally free to sing your very own dawn chorus of thanks and praise to Him . This is not only a song sung in triumph on the mountain tops. It is a song sung at the start of the exit from the grave and the valley of death's shadow.

Your song is a powerful weapon! When it is your very own hard fought for song, no season of darkness or triumph can take it away from you. It is a song that heralds His goodness despite circumstances. The bible is filled with psalms of praise when things have been going wrong, and yet the psalmist has chosen to give God the praise anyway. These 'and yet I will praise Him' psalms are victory anthems that chart the highs and lows (sometimes very lows) of living life with God. When I choose to praise God with my own song, even while in difficulty, then His glory is declared in my life, and His freedom breaks through and is present with me in those circumstances and in spite of them. Nothing can separate us from the love of God![5] There is such power in this revelation.

This understanding of freedom brings dawn to a new level. Our songs of praise to Him awaken the dawn and sunrise in our lives. Scripture is full of verses of thanks to God, ready for us to sing. As you step into your morning, find some scripture that you can use in your own song of praise to God.

Check your bearings

- ◦ Your song is a powerful weapon.
- ◦ Find some scripture that you can use in your own song of praise to God.

7. Packing Up

Our time in the campsite is almost over. Dawn has come, and it is finally time to pack up and head on to the next part of our journey. We have fought fear in the dark places, walked through grief and loss, and now started to more fully understand who we are in Christ. We have also discovered and started to sing our own song of praise to Him.

Karl and I have moved a fair few times in our lives. Some of the moves were simply across town, while others were across the country, and one trip across the globe. Moving is never easy, no matter how far you are travelling. While it is exciting to think of the new places that you will get to experience, it still requires you to leave what you know and is familiar to you behind. It involves the clearing away of old treasures and clutter, boxing up of belongings, and fond goodbyes to special friends. It can also involve handing over our dearly loved homes with their wonderful memories to new families. To willingly move takes trust and confidence that you are going to a better place.

Back in Jeremiah we read;

But blessed is the one who trusts in the Lord,

whose confidence is in him[1]

But how exactly do we actively move into a greater degree of trust and confidence in God as we pack up and move out of the campsite season? This next section in our journey to living your wildly unbroken life will delve into this question. We will look at where our hope and confidence is grounded, and discover more about how scripture instructs us to grow in active trust of God.

In order to grow to trust someone, we first have to quantify whether that person is trustworthy.

Trustworthy can be defined as 'able to be relied on as honest or truthful.' Its synonyms can include: 'dependable, as good as one's word, tried and true, incorruptible, steadfast and unswerving'. Throughout scripture God proves Himself as trustworthy. When He says He will protect, He protects; when He says He will provide, He provides; and when He says He will guide, He guides. He also is true to His warnings. When He warns that the course of someones actions will lead to a dangerous place where our faith can be shipwrecked, sure enough, if we don't change course, that is what happens.

Often when travelling in uncertain environments we take a guide with us on our journey. These days that guide can be as simple as a SatNav, while at other times, when the GPS signals are low or the digital maps quality is inconsistent, we may need someone to come along with us who has personal experience of the environments we are about to travel. The Holy

Spirit and the community of the local church are our spiritual equivalents.

Would you take along on a dangerous journey a guide that you did not trust? I certainly would not! So then, if you would not take along a guide that is untrustworthy, how would you check the trustworthiness of the guide that you have? The best judge of trustworthiness is personal experience. Either your own or others close to you with the track record of completing expeditions in the environments into which you are journeying. If you have been following along with me and joining in with the questions, and checking your bearing points posted at the end of each chapter, you will be able to refer back to the list of things you can be thankful for at the end of chapter five. Take a few moments now to pause and revisit those things you have written down. I am pretty sure you will easily see many times where God has proven His faithfulness to you, despite your circumstances.

In our lives I have seen time after time where God has gone before us and made the way ahead clearer, by little things He has done that have proven vital later on. One such time for us involved a client I had while working in business finance. This client had extensive and very specific experience in working with people with brain injury. I thought nothing of it until a year after I had stopped working with her, and Karl had finally been given the diagnosis of radiation induced brain injury. Her experience was vital in helping us to get the support we have needed. Without her help I would not have known how or where to access this support.

We can look again to the scriptures, and the story of Moses, to see another great example of God's trustworthy faithfulness, despite the circumstances in which Moses found himself. We also see the evidence of how God worked with the active trust given to Him by Moses. This trust was used to redeem Moses from a broken past and release him to set a whole nation free from slavery.

When we activate our trust in God a spiritual chemical reaction takes place that has the potential for explosive change in both our lives and the lives of those around us. Active trust involves us choosing to wholeheartedly engage with the work of God in our lives. It is not about us doing things for God, but letting Him do the miraculous in and through us. Another word for this active trust is faith.

Hebrews 11:1 says,

Now faith is confidence in what we hope for and assurance about what we do not see.

Faith pushes our own fear and comfort to one side in order to let God move. When we engage our faith we become conduits for the power of heaven to invade earth. The only limit is our willingness to engage with it. This is not ignoring fear in our lives. It is, however, about not letting that fear have the deciding word on our actions.

We all face fear at one point or another. Sometimes the fear is well founded because we have done things that are wrong, and are fearful of the consequences. Other times it's the fear of the unknown; where we have little or no control over the outcome. I think Moses faced both these fears when he was met by God at the burning bush. God called him to go back to a place he had run from, in fear for his life. He was fearful because he had murdered a man and been found out. Not a pretty past to go back and face. The penalties of this were very, very real. He was not being defiant of God because he was comfortable where he was. Let us be honest, a palace life was far more comfortable than the life of a shepherd. His defiance stemmed from the perceived consequences of facing his past and what he had done. Moses' time in Midian was a campsite season. But God called him back to his past because his future was to be launched in the place of facing what he had done wrong, and moving from his campsite to where God called him to be.

God had called him to be the one to lead his people out of the place of slavery to the place of liberation. But it took Moses to have the courage to face the place where his liberty could be removed, and have himself placed into that place of slavery or even death. So what does God say to the fearful if not curious Moses? It was, after all, his curiosity that had him looking in the place of danger at the burning bush. He also went looking for his people at work all those years earlier, before he committed the murder.

In the burning bush interaction between God and Moses,[2] God gave him some challenges that I believe He asks all of us when leaving our campsites. These three things say as much about human nature when facing the unknown as they do about God's character in the unknown.

The first challenge is about God being our provider. God asked Moses, 'What is in your hand?'

Moses' response was, 'A staff.'

The first challenge I believe God asks us is, 'What are you holding?' What opportunities, jobs and resources has He placed in our hands? For Moses it was as simple as a shepherd's staff. However that staff was more than just a simple stick. It had become part of his identity and his security. It was his job, and represented his ability to provide for his family. It was also his safety as a weapon when in the desert places, as well as the method with which he could protect his sheep. And God asked him to put it down. As he put it down, it turned into a snake. Scary times!

God knows the resources He has given you. He knows how they are a good thing for you when you use them for His purposes. But He also knows that these resources can be a danger to us when we let them define our future. As the staff turned into a snake, I think God was warning Moses that his provision and protection needed to be founded in God, and not in his own resources and abilities. When the staff was submitted to God's will and purpose, Moses was able to once again pick it up and use it as a staff. We all have resources at our disposal. These resources belong to God first of all, and are not solely ours. Are there areas of your life where you have held on so tightly to the resources that God has given you that they in turn have stopped you entering into His next best for you? These resources have the potential to become like a dangerous snare or venomous snake in your life.

The second challenge revolves around God being our protector. This time God asked Moses to, 'Put your hand inside your cloak.' When we are faced with the unknown, it can be tempting to worry about all the things that can go wrong with our own person. What happens if I get ill? What happens if I can't afford to clothe or feed myself? What happens if…? Moses moves past the 'what ifs?', and does as God asked. His obedience landed up with him having a hand covered in leprosy. God then asked Moses to do the same thing again.

How many times, when faced with the choice, would we choose to do the same thing again, when the initial outcome was not as favourable as we had hoped? Would you really put your hand back in the place of harm? God's first challenge showed Moses that God could be trusted to care for him. He, after all, asked Moses to pick up a venomous snake by the tail. That would not have been the wisest choice in my mind, but it turned out alright. This time God had asked Moses to put his hand inside his cloak and it was definitely not alright! And now God was asking him to do it again. What was Moses to do? What would you do without the benefit of hindsight? Could he, and should he, trust that God could look after him when the circumstances were far less than favourable? Would God heal or harm? Would he even have a hand left this time round? Moses was forced at this point to trust God with his safety, knowing that it was not certain either way whether he would have a healthy hand at the end of it. We can often be faced with similar circumstances to this ourselves, when we face the battle of ill health. We can believe that God no longer wants to look after us because we are ill. He must have forgotten that we are here. Does He even care? Moses takes the difficult choice of trusting that God is who He says He is, and is able to protect and save him, so Moses places his hand back inside his cloak. It comes out clean and cured!

Sometimes in our walk with God we have to learn to trust God despite illness or financial difficulties. Psalms 23 is a great example of this in action.

Even though I walk through the darkest valley,

I will fear no evil, for you are with me;

your rod and your staff, they comfort me.[3]

We have to be willing to walk through the middle of the valley of death's shadow and not just skirt the edges, knowing that God is with us in it. God will sometimes take us down the darker routes of life in order to give to us greater depths of faith and trust in His faithfulness through it. The question we need to ask ourselves is are we willing to go into the place of illness, knowing that He is just as much there with us, as He is in the times of wellness we get to enjoy?

The last challenge facing Moses was when God asked him to trust in His sustaining power. Moses is told that he can take some water from the Nile River and, as he pours it onto the ground, it would turn to blood. This is a rather macabre and gruesome thought. I believe this last challenge for Moses was one of lesson and test. God knew the curiosity of Moses. He knew that He had already challenged him to do things that others may have thought stupid or unwise, and he had stepped out in faith and done it regardless. This last challenge could only be tested in Egypt on the bank of the Nile. This was not a challenge that could have been trialed in the desert of Midian in order to see if it would work. Moses had to step out and go back to the place it all started. He had to go back to the place he ran from in fear.

Water was a symbol of life. Particularly for those in the desert. This last challenge was one where God was asking not for a quiet and private display of faith, but a very large and loud display of faith in front of others. It was to prove to the elders of the Hebrew nation that God was powerful enough to disturb the sustaining water courses of the Egyptian powers. Water was not only necessary for the Egyptians to live, but it was also a powerful symbol in their faith and belief systems. The calendar was based on the seasons and the high and low waters of the Nile. Moses proving that the God of the Hebrews was powerful enough to not only sustain the Hebrews, but disrupt the sustenance of those in power over the Hebrews, would have been a hugely convincing sign for them. But Moses had yet to see God do it.

Moses had seen God turn his staff into a snake and back. He had seen his hand go from healthy to unhealthy and back again. But he had not yet witnessed this. He now had to choose to go into the place of danger and trust that God could and would do this for him. He had to trust beyond doubt that God was His provider, protector and sustainer. Can we say the same of God's movement in our lives?

I think we are ready to see the new day with what that brings. This campsite we've been inhabiting needs vacating so let's get going. Our expedition is not yet done, and its conclusion can only be found in the landscape beyond the tent pegs.

Check your bearings

○ Active trust is another name for faith.

○ Activating faith causes a spiritual chemical reaction in heaven that has explosive effects on earth.

○ When we engage our faith we become conduits for the power of heaven to invade earth. The only limit is our willingness to engage with it. The obstacle in the way of it is fear.

Ask yourself

○ Am I willing to trust God to be my provider, rather than trusting in my own strength? Are there areas of my life where I have held on so tightly to the resources that God has given me that they in turn have stopped me entering into His next best for me? How am I actively displaying this trust in my life today?

- Am I willing to actively trust God to be my protector, even if this involves walking through a few valleys in the process? How am I actively showing God my willingness to do this today?

- Am I willing to let God display His sustaining power through my life? How am I actively engaging in this today?

8. Staying Hydrated

There is nothing quite so uplifting as a drink of cooling water when you are thirsty on a long, hot journey. Water is the most refreshing drink that God gave us, and is essential to the success of our expedition.

Drinking salty water is not a good idea. It is a particularly bad idea if you are already thirsty when you drink it. Rather than hydrating the body, drinking salty water has the nasty effect of dehydrating the body, and leaving you with an intense thirst as your body tries to rid itself of the excess salt. The way to overcome this thirst is to drink more fresh water than the salty water you have already ingested.

It is the same when we are distracted by the offerings the World promises us while we walk through the tough times of life. The more we seek after them, the more they fail to satisfy, but instead leave us thirstier than ever.

We see this in the book of Ruth as we follow Naomi's story. Her struggle and pain could have left her questioning God's goodness and presence in her life. Where was He when famine hit her land, forcing her to leave home for Moab with her husband and two sons? Where was He when one by one the men and providers of her security were taken from her by death? Where was He on the long, dusty and dangerous road homeward?

I suspect she felt very alone. Abandoned by God and man and left destitute in a foreign land with no hope of help for her and her two daughters-in-law. Even her arriving back home was not a cause for celebration. She no longer felt that she was entitled to the name Pleasant (the meaning of Naomi) but was more suited to the name of Bitter (the meaning of the name Mara). Yet despite her trials and deep inner pain there was a glimmer of hope in her heart. A deep reminder of the inheritance that was hers as a daughter of Abraham still burned within her. I believe this hope is what sustained her as she nurtured the young Ruth, and guided her in the ways of Israel. It was this hope that sparked the confidence in Ruth to even believe that Boaz would look favourably on her and help her. Hope is contagious. When it is expressed with the backing of faith it changes the atmosphere around you, and positively influences those who spend time with you.

So where does Naomi find this hope in the dry and thirsty season in her life? I think she found her hope in her position as a daughter of Abraham. We too can find our own hope in our inherited position in and through Christ.

You can find many examples of the very real predicament of thirst in Scripture. Living in a rich land surrounded by both deserts and seas, Jesus understood this principle well. And it was not simply a theoretical understanding. He had endured a 40 day fast in the wilderness after His baptism, and with a wealth of scriptural references to hand He was well placed to use the idea of thirst in His teaching.

When Scripture speaks about water, it is not merely speaking about the stuff out of the kitchen tap or, in Jesus' case, the local well or spring. Scripture uses water to talk about eternal life, salvation and the Holy Spirit. As water is essential for our physical cleanliness and bodily health, so active engagement with the Holy Spirit is essential for our spiritual health. Just as fresh water is vital to an expedition into the wild, so the Holy Spirit is vital to our journey into living our wildly unbroken life. I believe the Christian heart cannot stay healthy in the long place of exploration without engaging with the refreshing presence of the Holy Spirit within it. You can see this when Jesus said,

Let anyone who is thirsty come to me and drink. Whoever believes in me, as Scripture has said, rivers of living water will flow from within them.[1]

In this passage He was referring to the Holy Spirit that was to come at Pentecost. Here we have the answer to our thirst. But how do we experience for ourselves these promised rivers flowing from within us?

If you pour water onto a really dry sponge you will find that it tends to wet the surface and then runs straight off without fully penetrating it. Likewise, the first time you use a new sponge it will float on top of the water. It takes you to crush and squeeze the dryness and air out of it for the sponge to start to absorb the moisture available to it. The same can be said for the dry ground in rain. If the ground is really dry and cracked, when rain comes, the water can flow across the surface and cause flash floods without being absorbed into the soil. What is needed in seasons of drought is not huge deluges, but persistent soft rain.

Psalms 23:2b-3a says,

He leads me beside quiet waters,

He refreshes my soul.

It is the same for us as we search for the refreshing and cleansing waters for the soul. We need to let the persistent soft rain of the Holy Spirit flow into our beings and be absorbed into the very core of who we are. Let His presence fill you, heal you, and restore you after your long and dry night season. There is no quick fix to this process. It takes the regular decision to stop and take time with Jesus and His Word. It takes determined discipline.

We have thought a lot in our journey about how being blessed is something we are, not something we have. Blessing is also not a formula, it is a relationship with Jesus that points heavenward. A foretaste and reminder of what is to come.

Paul, in his letter to the Ephesians, put it this way,

> *When you believed, you were marked in him with a seal, the promised Holy Spirit, who is a deposit guaranteeing our inheritance until the redemption of those who are God's possession —to the praise of his glory.*[2]

When we taint that foretaste with earthly flavours, wants, and desires we only get hungrier for the truth of heaven but lose our ability to taste the reality of Him. It takes the cleansing fresh water of the Holy Spirit to realign us to His heavenly truth and promises again. We have been given a truly glorious promise of a heavenly inheritance in Christ.

If the water in John 7:38 was promised to flow from within us, then there is a responsibility, once again, to share that refreshing blessing to the thirsty world around us. But it is only when we are continually being filled with the Spirit that we can pour it out to others.

Our inheritance is mentioned again in Ephesians where Paul states,

This mystery is that through the gospel the Gentiles are heirs together with Israel, members together of one body, and sharers together in the promise in Christ Jesus. I became a servant of this gospel by the gift of God's grace given me through the working of his power.[3]

Philippians reminds us of the importance of reflecting God's glory in everything we do when it talks about Jesus.

Who, being in very nature God,
did not consider equality with God something to
be used to his own advantage;
rather, he made himself nothing
by taking the very nature of a servant,
being made in human likeness.
And being found in appearance as a man,
he humbled himself
by becoming obedient to death —
even death on a cross!

Therefore God exalted him to the highest place
and gave him the name that is above every
name,
that at the name of Jesus every knee should bow,
in heaven and on earth and under the earth,
and every tongue acknowledge that Jesus Christ
is Lord,
to the glory of God the Father.[4]

We can learn from this that when we live in servant-hearted humility for God's glory, we start to own the blessing He purchased for us on the cross, and reflect His glory to the world around us. It is all for His glory and should always point back to Him. If we miss the importance of His glory, and start living for earthly pleasure and self, we break the supply chain of our inheritance. We can see this emphasised in Ephesians 3:14-21.

For this reason I kneel before the Father, from
whom every family in heaven and on earth
derives its name. I pray that out of his glorious

riches he may strengthen you with power through his Spirit in your inner being, so that Christ may dwell in your hearts through faith. And I pray that you, being rooted and established in love, may have power, together with all the Lord's holy people, to grasp how wide and long and high and deep is the love of Christ, and to know this love that surpasses knowledge—that you may be filled to the measure of all the fullness of God.

Now to him who is able to do immeasurably more than all we ask or imagine, according to his power that is at work within us, to him be glory in the church and in Christ Jesus throughout all generations, for ever and ever! Amen[5]

While I still believe that the evidence of blessing is not seen in having 'stuff,' I also don't want to ignore those elements in our exploration. God is able to accomplish infinitely more than we can ask or imagine,[6] and the storehouses of heaven are ready for our use,[7] but there is a caveat for their dispatch. It must all be to reflect His glory to the world around us. If our prayers for material wealth and comfort are more deeply about our own preference than for His glory to be revealed, then I think that we should not be surprised when we don't get what we ask for. James 4:2-3 says,

You do not have because you do not ask God. When you ask, you do not receive, because you ask with wrong motives, that you may spend what you get on your pleasures.

Remember, we are as much Christ's inheritance as He is ours.

I pray that the eyes of your heart may be enlightened in order that you may know the hope to which he has called you, the riches of his glorious inheritance in his holy people,[8]

With this in mind we need to ensure that our hearts are closely linked to the heartbeat of heaven in Christ. The Holy Spirit is our heavenly counsellor. He gives us holy access to the heavenly courts to hear the will of God and Christ. When we start standing in this confident hope, we start to see with clarity the work God is doing in our lives, and our prayers start to line up with His will.

As we headed out of our own night season, packed up and got ready to move on, I realised how spiritually dry I had started to feel. I still took time out with Jesus, read my Bible and listened to worship music, but it was a step by step act of obedient faith rather than the hot blooded first love desire I used to have when I first became a Christian. I had to take steps I knew were right and healthy for me outside of my own desires.

This obedience really pays off. No, it is not always easy. Some days I have to stubbornly refuse to let my feelings get the better of me. There are some days I would rather spend an extra half hour in bed than get up and spend time with God. On other days I would rather watch something mind-numbing on TV, or play an idle game on my phone or tablet, than take some time to chat to God. Don't get me wrong. I do have a lie-in now and then. I am a fan of films and popcorn with the family, and know that there is no problem with a bit of 'me time' in my busy week. But when these desires take preference over my time with God, then I am on dodgy ground. These activities will leave me feeling dry and unfruitful if they totally replace my time with God.

Spending time with God is not some point scoring exercise done to prove my devotion to Him, for we know that we cannot earn favour with God by the works of our hands.

Paul says in his letter to the Ephesians,

For it is by grace you have been saved, through faith—and this is not from yourselves, it is the gift of God— not by works, so that no one can boast.[9]

And adds in his letter to the Galatian church that

The only thing that counts is faith expressing itself through love.[10]

In my obedience to seek His face when I did not feel like it, I contended for God to open my heart to the other people around me who were travelling the similar journey to us. I started to reach out and touch the lives of those around me who had not yet felt the touch of heaven on their lives. I deliberately chose to let the water of the Holy Spirit flow through me to impact those around me.

As I obediently stepped out into this, I started to come back to life once again. I have found that the more I have poured out, the more God has poured back into me. Once again, my first love for Jesus was reawakened in me, along with the fullness of His overflowing spirit.

The hand of heaven on our lives has been more evidenced through the people I have met than the stuff that I have received. And yet, even in this season God has still overwhelmed us with His provision. Not always the way I would have asked for, but in ways far more beautiful. We have met people I would have never met, and made friendships with people that I would break my heart if I had to do life without.

Prayer:

Dear God,

I am thirsty! Help me to taste the refreshing waters of heaven again. Realign my spirit to your heart's desire. When I am aligned to your heart, then I am free to receive the dispatches from heaven's storehouses. For your glory!

Amen

9. The Narrow Ledge

When we activate our faith we need to understand that we will face difficulties. This world wants to squash us and minimise the purposes of God within us. On our own we cannot stand up to this, but in Christ we have switched sides. We are no longer aligned or confined to this world, but to the Maker of Heaven and Earth, and He is victorious.

In John 16 Jesus says,

> *I have told you these things, so that in me you may have peace. In this world you will have trouble. But take heart! I have overcome the world.*[1]

Where there is a battle, there is a victory to be won. In our search for living our blessed life we can be so caught up in seeking our own comfort that we turn from the very thing that will push open the door to living in His fullness. Jesus did not shun the cross in favour of the easier path. He pushed headlong into His destiny, and won our victory in the process.

Sometimes what we perceive as the battle to take us out, is the battle to set us free! In Christ we are more than redeemed, we are victors with Him! He has made us new and saved us from the grips of death and hell. It is from this position that our redemption stands.

We read in the book of Ephesians,

Finally, be strong in the Lord and in his mighty power. Put on the full armour of God, so that you can take your stand against the devil's schemes. For our struggle is not against flesh and blood, but against the rulers, against the authorities, against the powers of this dark world and against the spiritual forces of evil in the heavenly realms.[2]

A civilian bystander to the battle does not put on the soldier's uniform. The only reason to put on the armour is if you are facing a battle. Our armour is found in Christ. We are told to be strong *in* the Lord and *in* His mighty power. The word to emphasise in this verse of scripture is 'in'. He is our strength and He has the power. The armour He gives us is not something that He gives us outside of himself. He is our armour!

The Apostle Paul also recounts the conversation he had with God about some of the battles he faced in his second letter to the Corinthians,

> *But he said to me, "My grace is sufficient for you, for my power is made perfect in weakness." Therefore I will boast all the more gladly about my weaknesses, so that Christ's power may rest on me.*[3]

We do not need to be strong enough on our own. It is in surrender to Him that we stand tall with Him and take the victory. This understanding gives us the courage to fight alongside Him. Not running from the battle in fear, but running into it with Him, already holding the certain assurance of our victory through Him.

Because of this assurance we can be certain that Christ stands in victory, with fear in a headlock. What confidence this should give us! Fear can accuse us, spit at us and whisper to our hearts. But Christ has fear in a headlock. He wants us to walk in His victory. He wants us to take charge over our fear. He is perfectly capable of defeating it on our behalf, but He wants us to stand with Him in victory. Not stepping into the victory as one who has been rescued but as one who has taken an active part to play in sealing that victory. He wants us to kill the ungodly fear in our lives with Him, and like David with Goliath, remove its head.

This path of active faith in our journey is like a narrow cliff edge path we get to walk. On one side is a steep drop and the other a sheer rock face. There is only one way to walk, and only one way to place our focus. If we look at the drop it leads to fear, and if we focus on the sheer rock face it leads to despair. The only option left to us is to look towards the path ahead, confident that the Holy Spirit who leads you onto His path can lead you through it to victory.

Activating our faith releases the power of God in us. If I truly believe something then I will take confidence in it. This confidence births within us a new hope.

Now faith is confidence in what we hope for and assurance about what we do not see.[4]

Fear and despair will try to block the vision that hope brings. They will tell you that what you are believing for is not possible. It will remind you of all the obstacles and 'what ifs?' around you. It will also offer you a compromise. Something that looks almost like the promise of victory we have in Christ, but that is not quite over the finish line and into the fullness of that victory.

There is a great example of this in Exodus, where you see the interplay between Moses and Pharaoh after yet another bout of plagues.[5] Pharaoh is getting really fed up with Moses, and calls him back into his presence. By this point, there have been many plagues, and the Egyptians' treatment of the Israelites has been getting increasingly hostile. The hostility has got so bad that the Israelites have started to lose their enthusiasm for the freedom God has promised them through Moses. Their conversation went something like this.

Moses and Aaron were brought back to Pharaoh. 'All right,' he told them, 'go and worship the Lord your God. But who exactly will be going with you?'

Moses answered, "We will go with our young and our old, with our sons and our daughters, and with our flocks and herds, because we are to celebrate a festival to the Lord."

Pharaoh said, "The Lord be with you—if I let you go, along with your women and children! Clearly you are bent on evil. No! Have only the men go and worship the Lord, since that's what you have been asking for." Then Moses and Aaron were driven out of Pharaoh's presence.[6]

Like the Israelites promise of freedom by God, have you ever been on the receiving end of a promise from God? Perhaps in those quiet moments of prayer when His voice touches your soul, or through the Word of God delivered to you from a trusted and faith filled friend? It is a wonderful and encouraging thing when that happens. The beauty is that we have all been given promises by God. The Bible is full of them.

The thing is, often those promised words to us also require some action on our side. It's not that we cause the word to come into being, as we know that it is by grace that we walk in His freedom and not by works.[7] We do however, have the responsibility to take ownership of His promises and to take steps to walk into them.

For example, if you have received a word from God that talks about you having the gift of pastoring people, and that God wants you to impact communities for Him through your interaction with people, it is far less likely to happen if you are living on a remote island as a hermit. This is an extreme example, but I think you understand my point. To walk into that word with Jesus you need to step outside of your front door, and more than likely move back into a community of more than one person. But what happens when we have received a promise and as we start to walk into it the fight starts and things get hard? Is it ever OK to settle for a part promise?

I think we all know what the 'correct' answer is to that one. 'No.' However I think we do this more often than we realise. We start to walk into a promise and then start to question ourselves as to what the promise really was, and therefore settle for a lesser promise. The danger with this is that settling for a lesser promise is in fact receiving no promise at all.

If we go back to our Moses versus Pharaoh exchange in Exodus 10:1-20, we can see this in action. Moses was faced with the choice of accepting less. He went before Pharaoh ... again ... to remind him that God wanted to release the people from Egypt to worship Him in the wilderness, and Pharaoh, as ever, said, 'No.' Moses goes on to tell Pharaoh that his lack of cooperation would cause yet another plague and catastrophe on Egypt. Pharaoh's advisors get a bit concerned at this and persuade the king to have another chat with Moses about the terms of his request. This is where things get interesting. Moses lets Pharaoh know again the terms of the agreement, and Pharaoh asks for some clarifications.

'So who do you actually want to take…?'

'Everyone.'

'What! No way... The men can go but the rest stay... That's what you asked for...'

The enemy has a clever way of making us second guess God's Word and accept a compromise. The serpent did it at the beginning in Eden with, 'Did God really say…?'[8] and Pharaoh is doing it now. He offers Moses a lesser choice; a 'some but not all of the promise' kind of choice.

I have faced these situations in my life. We were promised by God that He would help to clear a significant burden of debt from our family. This was at the time that we realised that Karl's recovery from the brain surgery was not going to go as we had hoped. He was getting worse and had needed to give up work. I had needed to reduce my contracted hours to care for him. We were in a financial black hole, and yet God clearly told us that He wanted to clear the debt. So we stood on the promised word and believed and confidently contended for it. By the end of that year, through multiple miracles and 'coincidences' the majority of the most crippling debts had been cleared. Oh how we celebrated! It felt like a real victory! However, the last of the debt, which was still significant, was still there.

This is where the doubts started. I started to challenge my memory of the promise. Did God say all of the debt, or just the most difficult and crippling bits? My doubt and confusion started to believe for less. We started to think that perhaps this last bit we needed to do ourselves.

I can see now that we were faced with a situation a bit like Moses. ' You can take the men but the women and children stay... that is what you asked for...' However, just like Moses I can see now that that was not what was asked for or what was promised. My heart had to stay steadfast on His promises, and know beyond a shadow of a doubt what my promise was. It is an all or nothing kind of deal.

My God does not make half promises. A half promise is an unfulfilled promise. Instead of accepting the half promise, we are starting to stand once again on the full promise. No compromise. No negotiating with the enemy. If God said He would do it all, then that is what He will do. I am so looking forward to the day when we celebrate the fulfilment of that promise. I know now more than ever that I will get that opportunity.

How do we make sure we don't settle for less? We need to get into the habit of reminding ourselves of His promises to us. Take confidence in His goodness and trustworthiness to fulfil them. Write down the words and promises He gives you. Make sure scripture is in every room of your home. Infuse every part of your life with those reminders of His promises. Then make your life a celebration to Him of the fulfilled promises around you. Constantly remind yourself of God's faithfulness. If He has done it once He can do it again.

Don't let despair and fear steal your faith. Hold fast to your hope and confidence remembering that God's words are sure, steadfast, and will not fail. In our Exodus story Moses did just this. He told Pharaoh that there was no discussion or negotiation in this matter. It was all the people or none of them. The narrow ledge of confident obedience. No compromise!

We all have our own promise from God that will require a no compromise attitude to fully take hold of it. What steps of confident obedience has Jesus challenged you to take or believe for?

Make a note of these in a journal or notebook. Perhaps share them with your climbing buddy. Making notes of your journey with God encourages your faith and that of others you meet. These little notes also remind you of your God promise. It's a whole lot easier to not accept a half promise when you have a record of the promise in full.

Check your bearings

- Sometimes what we perceive as the battle to take us out, is the battle to set us free!
- Fear and despair will try to block the vision that hope brings.
- God does not make half promises
- Write down your God promises so you don't accept a compromise.

10. Living in the Promise

So we step out and start to live and walk in the place of no compromise, believing God's promises; and things seem to get tougher. What then?

James describes a joy that is hard to stomach when in these situations. He calls it a pure joy.

Consider it pure joy, my brothers and sisters, whenever you face trials of many kinds, because you know that the testing of your faith produces perseverance. Let perseverance finish its work so that you may be mature and complete, not lacking anything.[1]

So when does your normal every day joy become a pure joy? James states clearly that it is in the facing of trial that perseverance is grown, through the testing of faith. The active faith we started to put to work earlier grows through perseverance.

Pure joy could be said to be distilled joy. This purity comes from the refining and distillation processes of life. How does this process happen? Distillation is the process of boiling a liquid down to its essence and most important part. As the liquid is heated the impurities are separated from the liquid as it turns into steam. When the steam is cooled down it turns back into liquid, but this time in a purer and cleaner state with less impurities. The more the process is repeated, the greater the purity. Distillation is used regularly in our modern world, and can be seen in the process of desalinating water, which is when sea water is turned into drinking water. It is also used in the making of some spirits like brandy and whisky.

The heat and difficult times in our lives can be seen as the distillation process at work in our lives. There is water in the saline. There is brandy in the wine. There is perseverance and greater faith in the trials and difficulties of life. We are challenged to cultivate joy in every circumstance. Enduring the heat, knowing that the end result will be worth it.

We can look again to the story of Moses as an encouragement during our pure joy, perseverance-growing seasons of life. I find his life particularly helpful in the times when I feel lost and forgotten by God. His story can act as a timely reminder that God's promises are sure and steadfast despite my circumstances.

In Exodus 6 we read the account of when God reminded Moses of the promises He made to Abraham, Isaac and Jacob. He tells Moses that He has heard the desperate cries of the people, and remembers the covenant promise He made to them all those years before. The promise was that He would lead them into a good land. He tells Moses all of this while the people of Israel are in the direst of oppression by the Egyptians, that has just been made worse by their request to leave to go and worship God in the desert for a few days. When we are in times of real struggle it is good to remember that God is still God, despite our circumstances.

Let's explore this in more detail. I have added some bold to the text to aid clarity.

> *Therefore, say to the Israelites: 'I am the Lord, and* **I will bring** *you out from under the yoke of the Egyptians.* **I will free you** *from being slaves to them, and* **I will redeem you** *with an outstretched arm and with mighty acts of judgment. I will take you as my own people, and I will be your God.* **Then you will know** *that* **I am** *the Lord your God,* **who brought you out** *from under the yoke of the Egyptians. And I will bring you to the land I swore with uplifted hand to give to Abraham, to Isaac and to Jacob. I will give it to you as a possession. I am the LORD.'*[2]

Reading from my NIV translation of the text, what I find really interesting in this passage are the tenses that are used.

- 'I will bring you; I will free you; I will redeem you' uses future tense.
- 'Then you will know' uses future tense.
- 'I am' uses present tense.
- 'Who brought you out' uses past tense.

God promised a future event as though it was already done. This does a huge amount for my faith in the tough times of life. Those times where I am still contending for the promises God has made to me to come about. His Word speaks to me that the promises He makes are not made in the same way as I make promises to my children. I could say to my daughter that when we go on holiday we will go scuba diving and have ice cream on the beach. I know that when I make that commitment I am going to do everything in my power to make it happen, while also being fully aware that it has not yet been done.

God's promises are different. That is because God sits outside of time. When He says that something will happen, in the heavenly places it has already happened. We are just waiting to see the physical presence of the promise on earth. When a woman falls pregnant, she becomes a mother. The child is already in her life. Most people she meets will have little or no idea for at least the first twelve weeks that the child is there and already growing. Just because a seven month pregnant woman cannot yet see and hold her baby, does it mean that the baby does not exist? No, it is just not yet seen or heard. The evidence of the child is there, but the physical presence has not yet made itself known. It is the same with the promises of God. Through the life, death, and resurrection of Christ the evidence of the promises God makes to us are there, but it may be that the physical fullness of all of those promises has yet to be seen. The promise is not voided just because we cannot yet see it.

I think this principle is really important in our relationship with God. He does not make promises to us from inside of time and space, therefore constraining them to the physicality of time itself. He makes promises to us from the heavens that sit outside of time and space. This means that when the Word says that with God all things are possible[3] it is true, because God's promises and abilities are not confined by the earthly physics of time and space. It also means that they cannot always be explained. God can most certainly use the scientific rules He created, but He is above being confined to them or by them.

In our earthy skin with its desires we are in confinement to time and space. However, in our freedom in Christ, with the newness and life that comes from Him, we are released from those confines. This can really help us to understand that when Jesus said, *'I will do whatever you ask in my name, so that the Father may be glorified in the Son'*[4] it really means just that.

Because of Christ our prayers can punch through the barriers and confines of time and space, and call heaven into earth. Because of Christ we are freed from our sinful nature and its desires. This freedom ever increasingly transforms us into the likeness of Christ.

This transformation means that our prayers, when made from that place in Christ, should be grounded on the principles of Heaven. One of those principles is selflessness. It is the is the purest form of love, and a foundation of the character of Christ. In contrast, our earthly principles are based on self and selfishness. Prayers formed on the principles of heaven will be answered with a 'Yes' from God, because they are formed straight from His heart and bring Him glory. When we pray from earthly spaces and perspectives our prayers are tainted by earth and its ways. I believe these prayers are far less powerful. This does not make them powerless, just less powerful. The Bible says that the prayers of a righteous man are both powerful *and* effective.[5] This means that they not only stop the forces of darkness in their tracks (that is the powerful bit) but also cause heaven to move on earth, affecting change (that is the effective bit).

I want my prayers to be founded from the righteousness of Christ, made in the heavenly places with heavenly grace and authority. I want to see God being glorified on earth! This means more to me than the shopping list prayers of selfish fulfilment. It changes the way I ask for health, prosperity and healing in my prayers. My prayers need to be made from a place of seeing the kingdom of heaven advance in the earth. These prayers push back death and darkness and usher in His kingdom. I am no longer constrained by my skin, so my effectiveness in service to God does not depend on the health of my body, but the health of my soul. Please understand that I am not advocating an unhealthy lifestyle that leads to an early death when I say this. That is a decision made while under the control of my flesh, and in selfish disobedience to Christ. Not taking care of my body is a selfish and irresponsible thing to do. That being said, my bodily health is not the thing that will impact what God can or cannot do with me. It is also not the evidence of righteousness within me.

When we pray from the heavenly perspective our prayers for healing become prayers of thanksgiving for the healing that has already taken place in the heavenlies, but perhaps not yet seen on the earth. Our prayers for jobs and finances become less of a desperate plea for release from our difficulties, but instead become prayers of praise to God for His faithfulness in the earthly waiting. This change in our attitude of prayer goes deep into the heart, and leads to a life of real joy, despite the circumstances we can see. This is because we *know* that God has heard our prayers and *has already* worked on our behalf. We start to live lives of real joy, despite suffering, struggle and pain, because we understand where we sit in Christ, and are looking forward with expectation to what is to come. We get the childhood excitement of Christmas in our hearts, knowing that what was on the wants list is under the tree waiting for the day we get to unwrap it! What joy and excitement that brings!

And that is the position and inheritance we get to have in Christ. Thank you Jesus!

Check your bearings

- ○ The promises of God are not voided just because we cannot yet see them.
- ○ Prayers formed on the principles of heaven will be answered with a 'Yes' from God
- ○ My effectiveness in service to God does not depend on the health of my body, but the health of my soul.

11. Cultivating the Land

It is one thing to be blessed. It is entirely another to live in that blessing. A rich man can live in squalor or in a mansion. It is not his wealth that holds him back or encourages him forward, but his use of that wealth. It is the same with living the wildly unbroken life with God. It is about understanding our position and inheritance in Christ, and of living in its fullness. We are called to live lives worthy of Christ,[1] so using Christ as our example is a great place to start.

The Apostle James wrote,

> As the body without the spirit is dead, so faith
> without deeds is dead.[2]

However, Paul in his letter to the Ephesians reminds us,

> *For it is by grace you have been saved, through faith—and this is not from yourselves, it is the gift of God—not by works, so that no one can boast.*[3]

How do we marry these two points together? I think we need to go back again to the promise of God to Adam, Abraham, Isaac and Jacob. They were blessed, and then told that the whole earth would be blessed through them. Remember that this does not mean that we have to strive for grace and blessing by doing. Instead, the gift of grace came first and the gratitude response to this grace is to pour more of God's blessing to the world around us. We become so full with the blessing of Christ, that the pouring of that blessing is a grateful response resourced from an overflow of His goodness, rather than from us striving and hoping that we have enough to go around ourselves.

This heavenly outpouring of blessing could also be likened to the workings of an electric circuit. The circuit can be connected to the battery terminal at one end, but unless it is completed at the other end, it won't work. Likewise, if it is connected to both battery terminals but there is no resistor in the flow of the current, be it a light bulb or other power using device, the circuit will short and sparks will fly. The same can be said for living in the flow of God's blessing in our wildly unbroken life.

Living in our blessed life means we need to understand the flow of the heavenly economy. If we seek to keep the blessing for ourselves, rather than pouring it out to others, it can be a destructive force in our lives. God wants the best for us, so will be reticent of turning on the power we have full access to if it will cause us damage.

You do not have because you do not ask God. When you ask, you do not receive, because you ask with wrong motives, that you may spend what you get on your pleasures.[4]

We are called to be the conduit for God's blessing to the world, and we have within us the potential to link the storehouses of heaven into the world. Blessing is a means for God impacting His world. Like a tree that bears fruit, we were never meant to hold on to it, but to pass it on. A tree does not bear fruit for its own benefit. It bears fruit to feed those who live in its shade, and to propagate more trees. If we try to live the blessed life just for ourselves, we minimise the impact that the fruit we bear can make.

When our lives are aligned to the calling that Christ has given us, we no longer live for ourselves, but for Him. Our purpose, vision and enthusiasm for the work ahead are not bound up by obligation or selfish desires, but by a deep love and devotion to Jesus. The purpose we have becomes a work of joy, much like the work that God had for Adam and Eve in the garden of Eden, before the Fall. This is truly the start of living the unbroken life. It is a life not holding on to self but a life poured out to others. Galatians describes it beautifully.

> *You, my brothers and sisters, were called to be free. But do not use your freedom to indulge the flesh; rather, serve one another humbly in love.*[5]

We have just looked at our heavenly source of refreshment, the confidence we have in our position in Christ, and the power this gives us in prayer. But we need to take this one step further. The Bible says that *'faith by itself, if it is not accompanied by action, is dead.'*[6]

This next place is taking this godly confidence and prayer to a new level, and start affecting real change in the world around us. It is the place of living with one foot in heaven and one foot on earth. This can be hard when life feels like it has put you in a corner, and there is nowhere to turn. But God always provides a way where there seems to be no way forward. Raise your head, mighty faith warrior, and see God at work. Then stand up, get your fight on and get your knuckles out.

This expedition we have gone on was never meant to be a gentle stroll into the Word of God. It was always going to be an adventure, and all adventure will come with adversity. I have really had to fight for this chapter of this book and it has not been an easy one to write. I am by nature a peace-loving person, who likes to get on with everyone. Don't get me wrong, I will fight in prayer and take down strongholds in the hard and lonely places of my prayer closet, and I have seen the effect of these prayers in powerful ways. However, if you ask me to physically speak up, or stand against a wrong-doing against me or the causes close to my heart, my default is to rather run and hide. But this character trait is not one that has been a true and full reflection of the confidence I have in Christ. As we saw in the last few chapters, God is into growth and maturity, so

He has taken me to the place where I have had to learn to fight for it.

When you fight in the physical places for the promised blessing of the heavenly spaces you start to pull together the completeness of living your blessed life. The joy is that God never asks you to fight alone. In our current fight we have had to start to enter the courtrooms of the world to fight for justice where wrongs have occurred. My authority in the courtrooms of heaven is clear and unchallenged in those places, because of my position in Christ. My authority in the courtrooms of earth, however, is a different matter. God has brought into our lives people qualified and authorised to work in these places. I have been challenged to take action both in heaven and on earth, knowing that my God fights for me, and will place before me the people that I need to fight with me.

This does not nullify my requirement to step up and call an injustice for what it is. It takes courage to speak up about where the wrong has occurred, and to relive the pain of the events that took place. We have previously walked through the challenges of grief and loss. This journey has been one of living out forgiveness. Forgiveness is not about ignoring justice, but it is about letting go of our right to that justice, and letting God deal with it. There is a healing that comes when justice is fought for. This healing requires you to speak up about the wrong, and give the pain and hurt to God in the process. If I hold on to the pain, no earthly judgement that is declared will make it right. But if I leave the pain with Jesus, and let His forgiveness flow through me, then the fullness of His healing passes through me and makes the justice compete.

This is one of the essences of living the blessed life. It is remembering that in every part of our journey the blessed life can only be lived in its fullness in the place of letting heaven flow through my life, to impact the world around me.

Let us look back again at the scripture we read at the start of our journey into living the blessed life.

> *But blessed is the one who trusts in the Lord,*
> *whose confidence is in him.*
> *They will be like a tree planted by the water*
> *that sends out its roots by the stream.*
> *It does not fear when heat comes;*
> *its leaves are always green.*
> *It has no worries in a year of drought*
> *and never fails to bear fruit.*[7]

The tree in Jeremiah produced fruit no matter the season. Fruit is grown on a tree for the purpose of releasing it to bless and nourish those around it. Trees are made to release. The fruit was never meant to be kept on the tree. The tree in Jeremiah was made to bear and release fruit no matter the season. We were made to bear fruit, no matter the season.

Check your bearings

○ What have you planted in your journey to living your blessed life, and what fruit are you producing? Is it the fruit of living your blessed life, because you will always harvest what you plant?

○ The seed your fruit leaves behind has the potential to produce more trees that produce more fruit. The further your fruit goes, the further the impact of living your blessed life will go.

12. One Step Further

Adventures leave you changed. The old life you had will never satisfy once you have tasted the wild and free adventure that is your life with Jesus. Our journey together is coming to an end, but that does not mean the adventure is done. There is always one more step to take. Jesus is always looking to grow you into a clearer reflection of Himself so that the world will be fully blessed through Him. There is always the call to go one step further. But will you accept the call, or will we shrink back to a lesser life? The call is powerful, and the journey ahead won't be easy. It will be full of rewards and heavenly treasure, but the choice is ultimately yours.

Imagine for a moment that you decided to cook an elaborate three course dinner for your family. You get up early and start to prepare the food, and finally sit down to serve it many hours later. You then spend another few hours doing all the cleaning, tidying and washing up, to restore your kitchen to the sparkling state it was before you began. Finally, in the late afternoon, you head into the lounge for a nice cup of tea, and rest with your family. From across the room pipes up a voice with the question,

'That dinner was lovely. What's for tea? Same again?'

I can honestly say that I think I know what my response to that question would be. And it would not be the holiest moment of my day!

With that in mind, now take yourself to the events retold in Luke's[1] gospel of the calling of the Apostle Peter, and put yourself in his shoes as you read.

You had just spent all night in a fishing boat, trying to catch fish to feed the family. By morning, the nets are empty and you have caught nothing except the rocks of the seabed that have broken and torn your nets. Tired from the long night, you call it a day, and moor your boat on the shore. Next comes the long and thankless job of cleaning and fixing your broken, empty nets.

As you get to work the new local celebrity, Jesus, comes along, followed by a huge crowd. The crowd is so enthusiastic to hear him speak that Jesus asks you if he can use your boat for a bit. Oh, and while you are at it, would you mind pushing it a bit further into the water so he can speak to the people from a safe distance? You get up, tired from work, but do as requested before going back to your nets. No one mentions how long Jesus spoke for, but I can only assume it was not a quick ten minute sermon. Your nets are finally clean and mended. You are tired and want to go home to bed, but you can't, because your boat is not secure, because there is a man in it. So you wait for him to finish.

At last Jesus is done. He turns to you and mentions that you should cast your nets out again, as there is a catch waiting for you.

Does this man know what he is talking about? It is midday, the worst time for fishing, and you are tired! You have only just tidied up and he is asking you to start again...

Haven't you done enough already? You let him mess up your day. You loaned him your boat. You waited for him to finish. You just want to go home to bed, and he asks you to start fishing again. Now. Really?

Slightly grudgingly you head back out onto the waters and follow the instructions of Jesus. The result is a catch so big that your nets cannot handle it, and start to break. You call your friends on the shore to come and help, so that your boat does not sink under the weight of the catch. It's been the best catch of your life!

Then again Jesus asks you to go yet one step further. Leave it all behind and follow Him.

Jesus, again and again, asked Peter to go one step further. Beyond tiredness, lack of income, and brokenness. He asks the same of us too. At the end of Peter's fishing career, there was a full but very broken net.

Sometimes on our journey to the blessed life we are taken to the very ends of brokenness, for God to step in and remake us and our lives into something new, something wildly unbroken.

Peter's newness meant he had to leave what he knew and understood behind. Our newness meant that we had to leave jobs, career prospects, health certainty, and financial security behind. We have to choose every day to follow where He leads. There is no guarantee that we will reap the rewards of this in our earthly lives, but I am certain that we will reap the benefits in the one to come. We all have a choice as we step out, to remain full and broken, or live a life of pouring out the fullness of God to those around, us and in turn become unbroken; healed and whole in all He calls us to be. Our healing may not be the physical healing we seek and desire, it may be a wholeness and healing that goes far beyond the confines of our bodies. Our unbroken wholeness has the potential to impact the world around us and the generations beyond us.

We are called to continue to step out in our adventure with God. Always ready to go one step further. We were never created to be settlers. We were made to be adventurers, ever ready to journey forward with Him, and intentionally impacting the lives of those around us in the process. Our journey will see us become more and more unbroken as He draws us closer and closer into Himself.

Keep walking, Adventurer. This book may be finished, but your adventure has only just begun. The world will seek to break us to tame us. Jesus calls us to an untamed life. A life lived Wildly Unbroken.

With Thanks

This book has not been a single person effort. There have been a wonderful team of encouraging people around me to help get it off the ground and you all deserve thanks.

My first thanks go to my family and particularly Isabelle, my beautiful daughter. You have patiently walked this journey with your mum and dad and never stopped smiling in the process. Your love and humour have helped keep my light burning way into the night as I fought for the words in this book. I also want to thank my dad, Martin, and the proof reading ninjas, Jan and Angie. You humbly agreed to endure poor spelling, bad grammar and messy drafts in order to get this into print. I sincerely thank you for that!

Graphics for book covers in an artform in itself and one that I am blind to be able to do. Kezia, you are gifted beyond measure in all things visual. Thank you so much for doing the contents of this book justice with the wonderful cover. And lastly, to my family and friends (you know who you are, and there are too many to mention by name) who have journeyed this adventure with me with all its twists and turns. Jo, you pulled out of me what I did not know was there. For Jane and Dave, who walked the internal spiritual journey of the last few years with me. For Dave and Sarah, who stood with us, cried with us, and prayed with us the day we got the news of Karl's brain tumour. Finally for the army of prayer warriors who never stopped knocking on heaven's door for us. Helen, Julie, Andy and Erri, Angie, and Jan to name a few. My thanks go to you all.

Notes

1. Pack your bags, Explorer

[1] Jeremiah 17:7-8

2. Base Camp

[1] Genesis 13:16
[2] Genesis 22:17
[3] Genesis 12:1-3
[4] Matthew1:1-16
[5] 2 Corinthians 1:20
[6] Ephesians 2:8-9
[7] Deuteronomy 10:14
[8] Psalms 50:10
[9] Romans 5:8
[10] Matthew 28:18-20

3. The Climb

[1] Genesis 2:18

4. It's Getting Dark Out Here!

[1] Psalm 121
[2] Isaiah 41:10
[3] Psalms 36:5
[4] Deuteronomy 31:6

5. Night Time

[1] Romans 8:28
[2] Luke 13:34-35
[3] John 11:1-43
[4] Matthew 5:4
[5] Jeremiah 17:7-8

6. Sunrise is Coming

[1] 1 Peter 2:9
[2] Galatians 3:26-28
[3] Ephesians 3:6-7
[4] Psalm 65:8
[5] Romans 8:38-39

7. Packing Up

[1] Jeremiah 17:7
[2] Exodus 4:1-9
[3] Psalm 23:4

8. Staying Hydrated

[1] John 7:37-38
[2] Ephesians 1:13b-14
[3] Ephesians 3:6-7
[4] Philippians 2:6-11
[5] Ephesians 3:14-21
[6] Ephesians 3:20
[7] Matthew 18:18
[8] Ephesians 1:18
[9] Ephesians 2:8-9
[10] Galatians 5:6b

9. The Narrow Ledge

[1] John 16:33
[2] Ephesians 6:10-12
[3] 2 Corinthians 12:9
[4] Hebrews11:1
[5] Exodus 10:1-18
[6] Exodus 10:9-11
[7] Ephesians 2:8-9
[8] Genesis 3:1

10. Living in the Promise

[1] James 1:2-4
[2] Exodus 6:6-8
[3] Matthew 19:26
[4] John 14:13
[5] James 5:16

11. Cultivating the Land

[1] Colossians 1:10
[2] James 2:26
[3] Ephesians 2:8-9
[4] James 4:2-3
[5] Galatians 5:13
[6] James 2:17
[7] Jeremiah 17:7-8

12. One Step Further

[1] Luke 5:1-11

Jasmine Waldegrave